SOUPS

**GOOD
HOUSEKEEPING**

SOUPS

70+ NOURISHING RECIPES

★ GOOD FOOD GUARANTEED ★

HEARST
books

HEARSTBOOKS

An Imprint of Sterling Publishing Co., Inc.
1166 Avenue of the Americas
New York, NY 10036

ISBN 978-1-61837-231-4

Distributed in Canada by Sterling Publishing Co., Inc.
c/o Canadian Manda Group, 664 Annette Street
Toronto, Ontario, Canada M6S 2C8
Distributed in Australia by NewSouth Books
45 Beach Street, Coogee, NSW 2034, Australia

For information about custom editions, special sales, and premium and corporate purchases, please contact Sterling Special Sales at 800-805-5489 or specialsales@sterlingpublishing.com.

Manufactured in China

2 4 6 8 10 9 7 5 3 1

www.sterlingpublishing.com

GOOD HOUSEKEEPING
Jane Francisco
EDITOR IN CHIEF
Susan Westmoreland
FOOD DIRECTOR

Cover Design by Scott Russo
Series Design by Yeon Kim

CONTENTS

Chilled Caprese
Soup (page 119)

Foreword

Is there anything more welcoming than the aroma of a simmering soup? A staple of American kitchens, a hearty bowl of heart-warming soup can be just what's needed on a busy day. Easy to compose with pantry staples and fresh ingredients alike, many kitchen classics require few ingredients. Simply gather the essential ingredients needed to meet your family's tastes and you can create an easy yet versatile meal with a pot of soup.

Soups are great to have on hand in many situations. Whether its a chilly day or a hectic night for your family, a bowl of tasty soup chock-full of vegetables can constitute a balanced meal; plus soup is usually low-calorie and low-fat. Be prepared by simmering a soup on the stove top throughout the day. Then, when you are ready or a family member arrives home, a made-ahead meal, that tastes better reheated, will be ready to enjoy.

While soups are a perfect choice for family fare, don't forget to include them on the menu while entertaining. The perfect dish to accompany any gathering, soup is a no-fuss dish that everyone will enjoy. Serve a bowl of creamy vegetable soup at your next dinner party or put up a pot of luscious gazpacho at your next tailgate or backyard barbecue.

In the Good Housekeeping kitchens, we always say that you can tell the best recipes by the number of splashes on the page. We have selected our very favorite recipes to fill the pages of *Good Housekeeping Soups*. We hope you take this cookbook into your kitchen, use it to create wonderful memories for your family and friends, and leave splatters on every page.

SUSAN WESTMORELAND
Food Director, *Good Housekeeping*

Introduction

Simply Delicious Soups

Easy to make and full of flavor, soups are an American tradition that has survived through the centuries. These one-pot meals can adapt to the needs and tastes of the time, whatever they may be. In large cast-iron pots over open fires, colonists cooked whatever seafood or game they could find with any available vegetables and flavorings to provide the energy needed to survive in an unfamiliar world. A few centuries later, these early combinations have become regional classics across the country.

Eighteenth- and nineteenth-century immigrants brought European, Asian, and South American ingredients and recipes to our repertoire of slow-simmered sustenance. Twentieth-century conveniences such as the refrigerator, freezer, slow cooker, pressure cooker, and microwave have made a wider selection of ingredients available throughout the year and offer easier or faster methods of soup preparation. Twenty-first-century innovation has led to the creation of soup combinations that are in tune with the new millennium yet are as enticing and comforting as the originals that inspired them.

Good Housekeeping Soups brings you the best of all these possibilities: New World classics, international favorites, and the latest from today's most stylish tables. So get into the kitchen, pull out your biggest pot and a long-handled spoon, select some ingredients from your pantry and refrigerator, and start cooking.

Soup Means a Great Meal's on the Way

When you get down to it, soups can be made from an infinite pantry of ingredients and can provide a satisfying meal with only one pot to wash. Making soups is just about the easiest thing you can do in the kitchen. It requires very little equipment: You'll need a large, heavy stockpot, saucepan, or Dutch oven with a lid; a long-handled spoon; pot holders; and a cutting board and sharp knife to prepare the ingredients. You'll probably find that everything you need is already in your pantry or refrigerator. Preparing soups doesn't require any fancy cooking techniques: Just combine the required ingredients, simmer them for the prescribed time, and don't let them burn.

Soups are loosely defined as any kind of meat, fish, or vegetables cooked and served in a generous amount of liquid. Centuries ago people ate soups by sopping them up with bread. This way of eating soup supposedly contributes to the dish's name. Soups can be filled with chunky ingredients as are chowders or gumbos; pureed to the thick, satiny smoothness of a bisque; or completely clear like bouillon or consommé. And as for ingredients, the children's story *Stone Soup* reminds us that there is always something in the cupboard or refrigerator that can be used to make a delicious soup. Depending on their heartiness, they can be served as a first course or an entrée for lunch or dinner. While soups are usually served hot, there are some cool classics such as vichyssoise and gazpacho that can't be overlooked. Fruit soups are a refreshing exception to the definition. They are usually not cooked at all, provide their own flavorful liquid, and are as likely to appear on a dessert or starter menu.

Although making soups is easy, as we tested these recipes in the Good Housekeeping kitchens we discovered some ways to make the experience faster, easier, more economical, and always satisfying. Here are our thoughts.

Plan Ahead

- While low-sodium canned broths provide an essential head start on busy evenings, a supply of homemade stock in the freezer is worth spending a few hours on making on a winter weekend.
- Keep a container in your freezer and collect small amounts of leftover vegetables, meat, poultry, broth, and vegetable cooking liquid to add to your next pot of soup. Deglaze the pan in which you cooked burgers, steaks, or chicken; cool the liquid, and add it to your frozen soup collection.
- If your garden produces a surplus of tomatoes, peppers, celery, or green onions, rinse, pat dry, chop, and freeze them in ½ cup amounts. Add them, still frozen, to soups and stews. Use within six months.
- For soups, sauces, and stews, puree herbs in a blender or mini food processor with a little water. Freeze them in a small ice-cube tray. Once frozen, store the cubes in a freezer-weight zip-tight plastic bag. (Do not use this method with rosemary; the flavor will be too concentrated.)
- When preparing soups, double the recipe and freeze some for a busy evening. Cool the soup in containers, uncovered, at least 30 minutes in refrigerator or until warm. Cover containers tightly; label and freeze for up to three months.

Head for the Kitchen

- Read the recipe and check to make sure you have all the ingredients (or suitable substitutes) before you start cooking.
- Check the cooking time to make sure it fits within your schedule. You might want to prepare long-cooking soups the night before, so they can be pulled from the refrigerator and warmed in a hurry when you need them.
- Select a large, heavy cooking pot so the soup won't burn. Make sure the pot has an extra inch of bubble room at the top and a tight-fitting lid to prevent evaporation and loss of flavor.
- If you can't keep an eye on your soup, plan to prepare it in a slow cooker or in a Dutch oven or casserole with a lid in a 325°F oven.

- To ensure the best results, always use standard measuring equipment. Don't be tempted to use tableware for measuring; use standard dry measuring cups for dry ingredients, glass measuring cups for liquids, and standard measuring spoons when measuring tablespoons and teaspoons.
- If a recipe calls for fresh herbs and you only have dried, use one-third of the amount listed (e.g., for 1 tablespoon of a fresh herb, substitute 1 teaspoon dried).
- When using dried herbs, be sure they are fresh. It is best to buy the smallest container of dried herbs possible, as they begin to lose flavor as soon as they are opened. Dried herbs should be used within six months of purchase.

Simmer for Flavor

- Sautéing meat, vegetables, herbs, and spices gently before adding them to the cooking liquid will enhance their flavor. If they are to be added near the end of the cooking time, use a separate pan to sauté vegetables and herbs, and deglaze the pan with some of the broth so no flavor is lost.
- To brown the meat perfectly, dry the meat well with paper towels, heat a little oil until it's very hot, and add the chunks in small batches. This way, moisture can evaporate and the pieces will sear, not steam.
- Bring the liquid to a boil with the ingredients that will need the longest cooking time, then reduce the heat and cook gently until they are just tender. Then add quick-cooking vegetables and herbs, and cook just until they are tender.
- The easiest way to remove fat from soups is to chill them overnight and discard the layer of solid fat that forms on the surface. If you are in a hurry, you can remove fat from hot soup by placing ice cubes or several lettuce leaves on the surface for a few minutes then removing them.
- Serve hot soups in warmed dishes and cold soups in chilled dishes.

Garnish and Serve

As delicious as soup is, almost any bowl of soup will be enhanced by an added splash of color or a bit of extra flavor. Chopped fresh herbs are the simplest of all garnishes. Choose an herb that complements the soup's flavor and color. For the best results, chop or snip fresh herbs just before using. Pureed soups can accommodate other kinds of garnishes. The smooth texture of a pureed bean or tomato soup calls out for a sprinkling of grated Parmesan cheese or crumbled bacon. Pureed vegetable soups are often topped with a drizzle of heavy cream.

Supergreen Mushroom &
Orzo Soup (page 21)

1 | Vegetables

Vegetables add a bounty of fresh ingredients and nutrients to a pot of soup. So versatile, vegetables offer a unique flavor profile to each recipe. Whether simmered in a warm broth like Supergreen Mushroom & Orzo Soup or pureed and spiced like Curried Butternut Squash Soup, these various soups are comforting. But we haven't forgotten the favorites! Tomato-Quinoa Soup, Onion Soup with Parmesan Croutons, and Mushroom-Barley Miso Soup offer a familiar taste with a modern touch.

VEGETABLE **Broth**

This broth is delicious, nutritious, and great in soups, risottos, and sauces. The optional fennel and parsnip lend a natural sweetness and an additional depth of flavor. For an Asian-flavored broth, add minced lemongrass, minced fresh ginger, or chopped fresh cilantro.

PREP: 25 MINUTES   **COOK:** 2 HOURS
MAKES: ABOUT 6 CUPS

4   large leeks

2 to 4 garlic cloves, unpeeled

Salt

1   large all-purpose potato, peeled, cut lengthwise in half, and thinly sliced

1   small fennel bulb, trimmed and chopped (optional)

3   parsnips, peeled and thinly sliced (optional)

2   large carrots, peeled and thinly sliced

3   stalks celery with leaves, thinly sliced

4   ounces mushrooms, trimmed and thinly sliced

10 parsley sprigs

4   thyme sprigs

2   bay leaves

1   teaspoon whole black peppercorns

Ground black pepper

1 Cut off roots and trim dark green tops from leeks; thinly slice leeks. Rinse leeks in large bowl of cold water, swishing to remove sand. Transfer to colander to drain, leaving sand in bottom of bowl.

2 In 6-quart saucepot, combine leeks, garlic, 1 cup water, and pinch salt; heat to boiling. Reduce heat to medium; cover and cook until leeks are tender, about 15 minutes.

3 Add potato, fennel if using, parsnips if using, carrots, celery, mushrooms, parsley and thyme sprigs, bay leaves, peppercorns, and 12 cups water. Heat to boiling; reduce heat and simmer, uncovered, at least 1 hour 30 minutes.

4 Taste and continue cooking if flavor is not concentrated enough. Season with salt and pepper to taste. Strain broth through fine-mesh sieve into containers, pressing on solids with back of wooden spoon to extract liquid; cool. Cover and refrigerate to use within 3 days, or freeze up to 4 months.

EACH CUP: ABOUT 19 CALORIES, 1G PROTEIN, 4G CARBOHYDRATE, 0G TOTAL FAT (0G SATURATED), 0G FIBER, 9MG SODIUM.

MISO **Soup**

This light, spicy broth is brimming with fresh vegetables
and chunks of nutritious tofu.

PREP: 25 MINUTES   **COOK:** 35 MINUTES

MAKES: 6 MAIN-DISH SERVINGS

1   tablespoon vegetable oil

2   large carrots, peeled and thinly sliced

2   garlic cloves, minced

1   small onion, cut into ¼-inch pieces

1   tablespoon grated, peeled fresh ginger

½   small head napa cabbage (Chinese cabbage), about ½ pound, cut crosswise into ½-inch-thick slices (about 4 cups)

1   tablespoon seasoned rice vinegar

¼   teaspoon ground black pepper

1   package (16 ounces) firm tofu, drained and cut into ½-inch cubes

¼   cup red miso (see Tip), diluted with ¼ cup hot tap water

2   green onions, trimmed and sliced

1 In 5-quart Dutch oven, heat oil over medium heat. Add carrots, garlic, onion, and ginger and cook, stirring occasionally, until onions are lightly browned, about 10 minutes.

2 Add cabbage, vinegar, pepper, and 6 cups water; heat to boiling over high heat. Reduce heat to low; cover and simmer until vegetables are tender, about 20 minutes.

3 Stir in tofu and miso; heat through, about 2 minutes. To serve, sprinkle with green onions.

....

EACH SERVING: ABOUT 185 CALORIES, 14G PROTEIN, 13G CARBOHYDRATE, 10G TOTAL FAT (1G SATURATED), 2G FIBER, 510MG SODIUM.

TIP

Miso comes in a variety of flavors, colors, and textures that fall into three basic categories: red, which has a strong flavor; golden, which is mild; and white, which is mellow and slightly sweet. Miso can be purchased in health-food stores and Asian markets.

Mushroom-Barley
MISO SOUP

Simmer meaty shiitake mushrooms, creamy barley,
and vegetables in a broth made with miso.

PREP: 20 MINUTES **COOK:** ABOUT 1 HOUR
MAKES: 6 MAIN-DISH SERVINGS

1   package (1 ounce) dried shiitake mushrooms

1   tablespoon olive oil

3   carrots peeled and cut into ¼-inch pieces

1   medium onion, chopped

2   garlic cloves, minced

1   tablespoon grated, peeled fresh ginger

½   cup pearl barley

½   teaspoon salt

¼   teaspoon ground black pepper

1½ pounds bok choy, trimmed and chopped

6   tablespoons dark red miso

1   tablespoon brown sugar

1 In 2-quart saucepan, heat 4 cups water to boiling over high heat. In medium bowl, pour boiling water over dried shiitake mushrooms; let stand 15 minutes. With slotted spoon, remove mushrooms. Rinse to remove any grit; drain on paper towels. Cut stems from mushrooms and discard; thinly slice caps. Strain liquid through sieve lined with paper towels into 4-cup glass measuring cup. Add enough water to equal 4 cups; set aside.

2 In nonstick 5-quart Dutch oven, heat oil over medium heat until hot. Add carrots, onion, and mushrooms and cook until vegetables are tender, about 15 minutes. Add garlic and ginger and cook 1 minute longer.

3 Add barley, salt, pepper, reserved mushroom liquid, and additional 4 cups water; heat to boiling over high heat. Reduce heat to low; cover and simmer until barley is tender, about 40 minutes.

4 Add bok choy; heat to boiling over medium-high heat. Reduce heat to low and simmer, uncovered, until bok choy has wilted and is tender-crisp, 5 to 7 minutes, stirring occasionally.

5 With ladle, transfer ½ cup broth to small bowl. Add miso and brown sugar; stir until smooth.

6 Remove Dutch oven from heat; stir in miso mixture. (Never boil miso; its delicate flavor and nutrients will be destroyed by high heat.)

EACH SERVING: ABOUT 170 CALORIES, 7G PROTEIN, 29G CARBOHYDRATE, 4G TOTAL FAT (0G SATURATED), 6G FIBER, 985MG SODIUM.

Making the Most of Miso

Miso, the intense Japanese soybean paste that punches up soups and dressings, is coming into its own in American kitchens. A little goes a long way toward adding a wonderful depth of flavor to healthy foods.

Sold in small tubs or jars at health-food stores and Asian markets, this high-protein, peanut butter–like paste is made from cooked soybeans, salt, water, and koji (a mold cultivated in a barley, rice, or soybean base) and fermented for 6 months to 3 years. The type of grain base, amount of koji, and length of fermentation affect the color (from pale golden to dark brown) and flavor—sweet, mild, salty, earthy, or meaty. Textures range from smooth to chunky.

High heat and boiling change miso's flavor, so incorporate it into a dish near the end of the cooking process. To avoid undissolved clumps, blend a few tablespoons into hot water or broth first. After stirring diluted miso into a soup or stew, heat mixture only to a simmer; serve immediately.

Store miso in the refrigerator in an airtight container for up to 1 year.

Tomato Soup with
CUPID CROUTONS

Ladle up a little love. Our tomato soup is superfilling and loaded with vitamin C.

PREP: 15 MINUTES **COOK:** 30 MINUTES
MAKES: 4 FIRST-COURSE SERVINGS

2   tablespoons olive oil

1   medium onion, chopped

2   garlic cloves, chopped

3   cups lower-sodium vegetable or chicken broth, or 3 cups Vegetable Broth (page 14) or Chicken Broth (page 38)

1   can (28 ounces) whole peeled tomatoes

2   bay leaves

½   teaspoon salt

4   slices white bread

1   tablespoon butter

½   teaspoon sugar

¼   teaspoon ground black pepper

1 In 5- to 6-quart saucepot, heat oil on medium. Add onion and garlic; cook 10 minutes, stirring. Add broth, tomatoes, bay leaves, and salt. Heat to boiling on high. Reduce heat; simmer 20 minutes, stirring occasionally.
2 Meanwhile, trim crusts from bread. With heart-shaped cookie cutter, cut 4 hearts from bread slices; toast hearts. Stir bread scraps into soup.
3 Remove and discard bay leaves. Stir in butter and sugar. In batches in blender or with immersion blender, blend soup until smooth. Stir in ¼ teaspoon pepper. Serve topped with heart croutons.

EACH SERVING: ABOUT 220 CALORIES, 4G PROTEIN, 27G CARBOHYDRATE, 11G TOTAL FAT (3G SATURATED), 3G FIBER, 928MG SODIUM.

TIP

This soup makes a warm, satisfying snack to beat the afternoon munchies and avoid the call of the vending machine.

Onion Soup with
PARMESAN CROUTONS

For the richest flavor, slow cook leeks, shallots, and onions
until tender, sweet, and golden brown.

PREP: 35 MINUTES   **COOK:** ABOUT 1 HOUR 15 MINUTES
MAKES: 8 FIRST-COURSE SERVINGS

1   bunch leeks (about 1 pound)

2   tablespoons butter or margarine

1   tablespoon olive oil

3   large onions (12 ounces each), each cut in
half and thinly sliced

4   large shallots, each cut in half and thinly
sliced

Pinch of dried thyme

2   tablespoons brandy

3   cans (14 to 14½ ounces each) chicken broth
or 5¼ cups Chicken Broth (page 38)

1   teaspoon salt

¼   teaspoon ground black pepper

4   ounces French bread, cut diagonally into ten
¾-inch-thick slices

¼   cup coarsely grated Parmesan cheese

1 Cut off roots and trim dark green tops from leeks; cut each leek lengthwise in half, then crosswise into ¼-inch pieces. Rinse leeks in large bowl of cold water, swishing to remove sand. Transfer to colander to drain, leaving sand in bottom of bowl.

2 In 8-quart saucepot, melt butter and olive oil over medium-high heat until hot. Add leeks, onions, shallots, and thyme, reduce heat to low and cook, covered, until tender and deep golden brown, 40 to 45 minutes, stirring occasionally.

3 Remove cover and increase heat to high. Add brandy and cook, stirring until browned bits are loosened from bottom of saucepot, 1 minute. Add broth, salt, pepper, and 4 cups water; heat to boiling. Reduce heat to low; cover and simmer 20 minutes.

4 Meanwhile, preheat oven to 450°F. On 15½" by 10½" jelly-roll pan or on large cookie sheet, arrange bread slices in single layer; bake 3 minutes. Turn slices over; sprinkle tops with Parmesan cheese and bake until toasted, about 5 minutes longer. Top each serving with a Parmesan crouton.

EACH SERVING: ABOUT 135 CALORIES, 6G PROTEIN, 16G CARBOHYDRATE, 5G TOTAL FAT (2G SATURATED), 3G FIBER, 761MG SODIUM.

Supergreen Mushroom &
ORZO SOUP

This comforting, one-pot goodness takes advantage of ingredients you might have on hand. For photo, see page 12.

PREP: 10 MINUTES   **COOK:** ABOUT 30 MINUTES
MAKES: 6 MAIN-DISH SERVINGS

2   tablespoons olive oil

¼   teaspoon salt

1¼ cups celery, chopped

½   cup shallots, chopped

¼   cup garlic, chopped

8   cups vegetable or chicken broth, or 8 cups Vegetable Broth (page 14) or Chicken Broth (page 38)

3   cups broccoli, chopped

3   cups spinach, sliced

1   cup mushrooms, sliced

1   cup orzo, uncooked

Basil pesto, to taste

1 In an 8-quart saucepot, heat olive oil over medium heat. Add salt, celery, shallots, and garlic. Cook 8 minutes or until golden, stirring.
2 Add broth and broccoli. Heat to simmering on high. Reduce heat to medium-low; simmer 15 minutes, stirring occasionally.
3 Add spinach, mushrooms, and orzo. Simmer 8 to 10 minutes or until starches and veggies are softened.
4 Remove from heat. Stir in basil pesto to taste.

....

EACH SERVING: ABOUT 230 CALORIES, 7G PROTEIN, 34G CARBOHYDRATE, 8G TOTAL FAT (1G SATURATED), 5G FIBER, 360MG SODIUM.

TIP

Out of broccoli? Swap with cauliflower or root veggies such as squash or carrots. Leafy greens such as kale, collards, and chard can replace the spinach.

Savory Pumpkin & Sage
SOUP

This festive soup with an elegant sage and mushroom garnish
is perfect for entertaining.

PREP: 25 MINUTES   **COOK:** 1 HOUR 30 MINUTES
MAKES: 8 FIRST-COURSE SERVINGS

¼ cup olive oil

1¼ teaspoons salt

3 large sweet onions, sliced

3 garlic cloves, chopped

2 large fresh sage leaves, chopped

2 teaspoon grated, peeled fresh ginger

¼ teaspoon ground nutmeg

2 quarts lower-sodium vegetable or chicken
   broth, or 8 cups Vegetable Broth (page 14)
   or Chicken Broth (page 38)

3 cans (15 ounces each) pure pumpkin

1 tablespoon fresh lemon juice

¼ teaspoon ground black pepper

Sage & Shiitake Garnish

Olive oil

24 small fresh sage leaves

2 packages (3½ ounces each) shiitake
   mushrooms, stemmed and very thinly sliced

Salt

1 In 5-quart saucepot, heat oil over medium heat
until hot. Add onions and 2 teaspoon salt; cook,
stirring occasionally, for 40 minutes or until
deep golden brown. Add garlic, sage, ginger, and
nutmeg; cook, stirring occasionally, for 5 minutes
or until garlic is golden. Add broth and pumpkin.
Heat to simmering over high heat, stirring until
browned bits are loosened from bottom of pot.
Reduce heat to maintain simmer; cook , stirring
occasionally, for 20 minutes.

2 With immersion blender or in batches in
blender, puree soup until smooth. Stir in lemon
juice, remaining 1 teaspoon salt, and pepper.

3 **Prepare Sage & Shiitake Garnish:**
Meanwhile, in 2-quart saucepan, heat 1 inch
olive oil over high heat until hot but not smoking.
Add sage leaves and fry, stirring occasionally,
for 1 to 2 minutes or until leaves are browned.
With slotted spoon, transfer to large paper
towel–lined plate; sprinkle with pinch of salt. In
batches, add mushrooms to hot oil. Fry, stirring
occasionally, for 2 minutes or until deep golden
brown. Transfer to same plate as sage; sprinkle
with pinch of salt. Cool completely. Garnish can
be made up to 3 hours ahead. Let stand at room
temperature.

EACH SERVING: ABOUT 215 CALORIES, 5G PROTEIN,
32G CARBOHYDRATE, 10G TOTAL FAT (1G SATURATED),
9G FIBER, 750MG SODIUM.

TIP
This recipe can be prepared and chilled for
up to 2 days ahead. Reheat over medium heat.
Add water or broth for desired consistency.

Broccoli & Cheddar
SOUP

Served with homemade multigrain bread (or a bakery loaf) and a crisp salad, this rich soup makes a satisfying meal. Use a blender, not a food processor, for an extra-smooth texture.

PREP: 35 MINUTES **COOK:** 25 MINUTES
MAKES: 8 FIRST-COURSE OR 4 MAIN-DISH SERVINGS

1 tablespoon olive oil

1 medium onion, chopped

¼ cup all-purpose flour

½ teaspoon salt

¼ teaspoon dried thyme

⅛ teaspoon ground nutmeg

Ground black pepper

2 cups low-fat milk (2%)

1 can (14 to 14½ ounces) chicken broth or 1 ¾ cups Chicken Broth (page 38)

1 large bunch broccoli (1½ pounds), cut into 1-inch pieces (including stems)

1½ cups shredded sharp Cheddar cheese (6 ounces)

1 In 4-quart saucepan, heat olive oil over medium heat until hot. Add onion and cook, stirring occasionally, until golden, about 10 minutes. Stir in flour, salt, thyme, nutmeg, and ¼ teaspoon pepper; cook, stirring frequently, 2 minutes.

2 Gradually stir in milk, broth, and 1½ cups water. Add broccoli and heat to boiling over high heat. Reduce heat to low; cover and simmer until broccoli is tender, about 10 minutes.

3 Spoon one-third of mixture into blender; cover, with center part of lid removed to let steam escape, and puree until very smooth. Pour into large bowl. Repeat twice more with remaining mixture.

4 Return puree to same clean saucepan and heat to boiling over high heat, stirring occasionally. Remove from heat; stir in cheese until melted and smooth. To serve, sprinkle with coarsely ground black pepper.

EACH FIRST-COURSE SERVING: ABOUT 185 CALORIES, 12G PROTEIN, 12G CARBOHYDRATE, 11G TOTAL FAT (6G SATURATED), 4G FIBER, 485MG SODIUM.

Thai Coconut SOUP

Quick, exotic, and delicious, this soup is full of protein and flavor.

PREP: 15 MINUTES   **COOK:** 5 MINUTES
MAKES: 4 MAIN-DISH SERVINGS

- 2   small carrots, each cut crosswise in half
- ½   medium red bell pepper
- 1   can (14 ounces) light unsweetened coconut milk (not cream of coconut), well stirred
- 2   garlic cloves, crushed with garlic press
- 1   piece (2 inches) peeled fresh ginger, cut into 4 slices
- ½   teaspoon ground coriander
- ½   teaspoon ground cumin
- ¼   teaspoon ground red pepper (cayenne)
- 12   ounces firm tofu, cut into 1-inch pieces
- 2   cans (14 to 14½ ounces each) vegetable broth or chicken broth, or 3½ cups Vegetable Broth (page 14) or Chicken Broth (page 38)
- 1   tablespoon Asian fish sauce
- 1   tablespoon fresh lime juice
- 2   green onions, sliced
- ½   cup chopped fresh cilantro

1 With vegetable peeler, remove lengthwise strips from carrots and edge of red bell pepper. Set aside.

2 In 5-quart Dutch oven, heat ½ cup coconut milk to boiling over medium heat. Add garlic, ginger, coriander, cumin, and ground red pepper, and cook, stirring, 1 minute.

3 Increase heat to medium-high. Stir in tofu, broth, carrot strips, pepper strips, fish sauce, lime juice, 1 cup water, and remaining coconut milk; heat just to simmering. Remove and discard ginger. Stir in green onions and cilantro just before serving.

EACH SERVING: ABOUT 210 CALORIES, 11G PROTEIN, 14G CARBOHYDRATE, 17G TOTAL FAT (6G SATURATED), 2G FIBER, 1,060MG SODIUM.

Curried Butternut Squash
SOUP

The secret to making this low-fat soup thick and velvety smooth without a drop of cream is using a blender to puree the soup in small batches. It freezes very well: Reheat the soup directly from its frozen state when ready to serve.

PREP: 20 MINUTES **COOK:** 40 MINUTES
MAKES: 12 FIRST-COURSE SERVINGS

3 tablespoons butter or margarine

2 large onions (12 ounces each), sliced

1 tablespoon curry powder

2 large butternut squashes (3½ pounds total), peeled, seeded, and cut into ½-inch pieces

2 cans (14 to 14½ ounces each) chicken broth or 3½ cups Chicken Broth (page 38)

½ teaspoon salt

1 In 5-quart Dutch oven or saucepot, melt 2 tablespoons butter over medium heat. Add onions and cook, stirring occasionally, until golden and tender, 18 to 20 minutes. Add curry and remaining 1 tablespoon butter and cook, stirring, 1 minute.

2 Add squash, broth, salt, and 2¼ cups water; heat to boiling. Reduce heat to low; cover and simmer soup until squash is very tender, about 20 minutes.

3 Spoon one-third of mixture into blender; cover, with center part of lid removed to let steam escape, and puree until very smooth. Pour into large bowl. Repeat twice more with remaining mixture.

4 Clean Dutch oven and return soup to pan; heat through.

EACH SERVING: ABOUT 95 CALORIES, 3G PROTEIN, 15G CARBOHYDRATE, 3G TOTAL FAT (2G SATURATED), 3G FIBER, 351MG SODIUM.

Vegetable CHOWDER

If you have your own vegetable garden or if you live near a farmers' market, you will want to make this luscious soup to take advantage of the fresh summer produce.

PREP: 15 MINUTES   **COOK:** 30 MINUTES
MAKES: 6 MAIN-DISH SERVINGS

2   tablespoons olive oil

1   large onion (12 ounces), chopped

3   medium zucchini and/or yellow summer squashes (about 8 ounces each), coarsely chopped

2   red and/or yellow bell peppers, coarsely chopped

3   large ripe tomatoes (2 pounds), coarsely chopped

3   large garlic cloves, crushed with garlic press

½   teaspoon fennel seeds

2   teaspoons salt

¼   teaspoon ground black pepper

Sliced fresh basil leaves, for garnish

1 In 5-quart saucepot or Dutch oven, heat oil over medium-high heat. Add onion and cook until tender and lightly browned, about 10 minutes. Add 3 cups water, zucchini and/or yellow squashes, bell peppers, tomatoes, garlic, fennel seeds, salt, and black pepper; heat to boiling. Reduce heat to medium and cook, uncovered, until vegetables are tender, about 20 minutes. **2** Spoon one-third of the mixture into blender; cover, with center part of cover removed to let steam escape, and puree until smooth. Pour puree into bowl. Repeat with remaining mixture. **3** To serve hot, return soup to same clean saucepot and heat through. To serve cold, cover and refrigerate at least 4 hours. Garnish with sliced basil.

EACH SERVING: ABOUT 120 CALORIES, 4G PROTEIN, 18G CARBOHYDRATE, 5G TOTAL FAT (1G SATURATED), 5G FIBER, 795MG SODIUM.

Ginger Carrot SOUP

This creamy-smooth soup is supercharged with vision-enhancing vitamin A. Subbing ginger-steeped green tea for stock slashes sodium.

PREP: 25 MINUTES   **COOK:** ABOUT 30 MINUTES
MAKES: 4 MAIN-DISH SERVINGS

4   green onions

1   (1-inch) piece fresh ginger

3   green tea bags

1   tablespoon olive oil

1   medium onion, finely chopped

1 ½ pounds carrots, peeled and cut into ¾-inch thick pieces

1   medium all-purpose potato, peeled and chopped

½   teaspoon salt

¼   teaspoon ground black pepper

2   cups frozen peas

1 From green onions, cut off white and pale green parts and place in 5-quart saucepot. Thinly slice dark green onion parts; set aside. From ginger, cut 4 slices; set aside. Peel remaining piece of ginger and grate enough to make 1 teaspoon; set aside.

2 To saucepot, add sliced ginger and 5 cups water. Heat to boiling over high heat. Add tea bags. Cover, remove from heat, and let stand 10 minutes.

3 While tea steeps, in 12-inch skillet, heat oil over medium-high heat. Add onion, carrots, potato, and ¼ teaspoon each salt and pepper. Cook, stirring, 6 minutes or until golden. Add grated ginger; cook 1 minute, stirring.

4 With slotted spoon, remove ginger, tea bags, and green onion pieces from pot and discard after squeezing excess liquid back into pot. Heat ginger tea to boiling over high heat; stir in carrot mixture. Reduce heat to maintain simmer. Cook 10 minutes or until vegetables are tender, stirring.

5 Transfer half of soup to blender; keep remaining soup simmering. Carefully puree until smooth, then return to pot. Stir in peas and remaining ¼ teaspoon salt. Cook 3 minutes or until peas are bright green and hot. Divide among soup bowls; garnish with sliced green onions.

EACH SERVING: ABOUT 205 CALORIES, 7G PROTEIN, 37G CARBOHYDRATE, 4G TOTAL FAT (1G SATURATED), 6G FIBER, 410MG SODIUM.

Barley MINESTRONE

Top this soup with a dollop of our homemade pesto, which you can make in a mini food processor. No mini processor? Store-bought refrigerated pesto makes an excellent stand-in—although it's not as light as our version.

PREP: ABOUT 25 MINUTES   **COOK:** ABOUT 50 MINUTES
MAKES: 6 MAIN-DISH SERVINGS

1   cup pearl barley

1   tablespoon olive oil

2   cups thinly sliced green cabbage (about ¼ small head)

2   large carrots, each cut lengthwise in half, then crosswise into ½-inch-thick slices

2   large stalks celery, cut into ½-inch dice

1   medium onion, cut into ½-inch dice

1   garlic clove, finely chopped

2   cans (14 to 14½ ounces each) vegetable broth or 3½ cups Vegetable Broth (page 14)

1   can (14 to 14½ ounces) diced tomatoes

¼   teaspoon salt

1   medium zucchini (about 6 ounces), cut into ½-inch dice

¼   pound green beans, cut into ½-inch pieces (about 1 cup)

1 Heat 5- to 6-quart Dutch oven over medium-high heat until hot. Add barley and cook 3 to 4 minutes or until toasted and fragrant, stirring constantly. Transfer barley to small bowl; set aside.

2 In same Dutch oven, heat oil over medium-high heat until hot. Add cabbage, carrots, celery, and onion; cook 8 to 10 minutes or until vegetables are tender and lightly browned, stirring occasionally. Add garlic and cook 30 seconds or until fragrant. Stir in barley, 3 cups water, broth, tomatoes, and salt. Cover and heat to boiling over high heat. Reduce heat to low and simmer, covered, 25 minutes.

3 Stir zucchini and beans into barley mixture; increase heat to medium and cook, covered, 10 to 15 minutes longer until all vegetables and barley are tender.

4 Ladle minestrone into 6 large soup bowls. Top each serving with some pesto.

EACH SERVING SOUP WITHOUT PESTO: ABOUT 215 CALORIES, 7G PROTEIN, 42G CARBOHYDRATE, 4G TOTAL FAT (0G SATURATED), 9G FIBER, 690MG SODIUM.

Light PESTO

1   cup firmly packed fresh basil

2   tablespoons olive oil

¼   teaspoon salt

¼   cup freshly grated Parmesan or Pecorino Romano cheese

1   garlic clove, finely chopped

In a blender container with narrow base, or in mini food processor, combine basil, oil, 2 tablespoons water, and salt; cover and blend until mixture is pureed. Transfer pesto to small bowl; stir in Parmesan and garlic. Makes about ½ cup.

EACH TEASPOON PESTO: ABOUT 15 CALORIES, 0G PROTEIN, 0G CARBOHYDRATE, 1G TOTAL FAT (0G SATURATED), 0G FIBER, 35MG SODIUM.

Tomato-Quinoa SOUP

Protein-packed quinoa is the perfect addition to this fresh, brightly flavored, and meatless soup.

PREP: 15 MINUTES **COOK:** ABOUT 15 MINUTES
MAKES: 6 MAIN-DISH SERVINGS

1 cup red or white quinoa, rinsed

3 tablespoons butter

1 tablespoon olive oil

2 medium shallots, chopped

2 garlic cloves, chopped

1 tablespoon fennel seeds

2 cans (28 ounces each) whole peeled tomatoes

2 cups lower-sodium chicken or vegetable broth, or 2 cups Chicken Broth (page 38) or Vegetable Broth (page 14)

¼ cup roasted salted pepitas (pumpkin seeds)

1 tablespoon snipped fresh chives

½ teaspoon crushed red pepper

1 Cook quinoa as label directs.

2 In 4-quart saucepan, heat butter and oil on medium heat until butter melts. Add shallots, garlic, and fennel seeds. Cook 4 to 6 minutes or until vegetables begin to soften, stirring occasionally. Add tomatoes and broth. Heat to simmering on high. Simmer 15 minutes, stirring occasionally. With immersion or regular blender, puree mixture until smooth. Reheat soup if necessary.

3 In medium bowl, combine cooked quinoa, pepitas, chives, and crushed red pepper. Serve soup topped with quinoa mixture.

EACH SERVING: ABOUT 275 CALORIES, 9G PROTEIN, 34G CARBOHYDRATE, 13G TOTAL FAT (5G SATURATED), 7G FIBER, 875MG SODIUM.

Caldo VERDE

In Portugal, this delicious soup gets its rich green color from finely shredded Galician cabbage. Kale, readily available in supermarkets, makes a fine substitute.

PREP: 25 MINUTES   **COOK:** 35 MINUTES
MAKES: 5 MAIN-DISH SERVINGS

2   tablespoons olive oil

1   large onion (12 ounces), finely chopped

3   garlic cloves, minced

2½ pounds all-purpose potatoes (about 8 medium), peeled and cut into 2-inch pieces

2   cans (14 to 14½ ounces each) chicken broth or 3½ cups Chicken Broth (page 38)

1   teaspoon salt

¼   teaspoon ground black pepper

1   pound kale, tough stems and veins trimmed and leaves very thinly sliced

½   cup linguiça or chorizo (optional)

1 In 5-quart Dutch oven, heat oil over medium heat. Add onion and garlic; cook until lightly browned, about 10 minutes.

2 Add potatoes, broth, salt, pepper, and 3 cups water; heat to boiling over high heat. Reduce heat to low; cover and simmer until potatoes are fork-tender, about 20 minutes.

3 With potato masher, mash potatoes in broth until potatoes are lumpy.

4 Stir in kale; simmer, uncovered, until tender, 5 to 8 minutes. Garnish with the linguiça or chorizo, if you like.

EACH SERVING: ABOUT 250 CALORIES, 8G PROTEIN, 42G CARBOHYDRATE, 7G TOTAL FAT (1G SATURATED), 7G FIBER, 925MG SODIUM.

New Orleans GREEN GUMBO

Popular around the Mississippi Delta, this soup has a slightly thickened "gumbo" texture created by the pepper-spiked brown roux and grated potato.

PREP: 40 MINUTES **COOK:** 20 MINUTES
MAKES: 8 FIRST-COURSE SERVINGS

8 slices bacon, cut into ½-inch pieces

¼ cup all-purpose flour

1 teaspoon salt

¼ teaspoon ground red pepper (cayenne)

2 cans (14 to 14½ ounces each) chicken broth or 3½ cups Chicken Broth (page 38)

1½ pounds fresh greens (collard or mustard, or a combination), tough stems trimmed and leaves cut into ½-inch pieces

1 package (10 ounces) frozen chopped spinach, thawed

1 large all-purpose potato (8 ounces), peeled and grated

1 In 5-quart Dutch oven, cook bacon over medium-low heat until browned. With slotted spoon, transfer to paper towels to drain. Set aside.

2 Discard all but 2 tablespoons bacon drippings from Dutch oven. Stir in flour, salt, and ground red pepper and cook over medium heat, stirring frequently, until golden brown, about 5 minutes.

3 Stir in broth, fresh greens, spinach, potato, and 4 cups water; heat to boiling over high heat. Reduce heat to low; cover and simmer, stirring occasionally, until soup thickens slightly and greens are tender, 20 to 25 minutes. To serve, sprinkle with bacon.

....

EACH SERVING: ABOUT 145 CALORIES, 7G PROTEIN, 14G CARBOHYDRATE, 7G TOTAL FAT (3G SATURATED), 4G FIBER, 735MG SODIUM.

TIP
Wash and cut greens a day ahead; store, loosely wrapped, in the refrigerator.

Lemon-Dill Chicken
Meatball Soup (page 42)

2 | Poultry & Meat

What's better than soup after a chilly day? A warm bowl filled with delicious ingredients like chicken and beef will always hit the spot. Plus, these soups make an easy dinner solution for busy weeknights.

Ladle up a classic like our Chicken Noodle or Country Beef & Veggie Soup. Want more variety? We offer some heat with Southwestern Chicken Soup and global flavors in our Thai Chicken-Basil Soup. Plus, a bowl of Chicken & Bacon Chowder will stick to your bones. These recipes are the definition of comfort food.

Chicken BROTH

Nothing beats the flavor of homemade chicken broth.
Make it in large batches and freeze in sturdy containers for up to
four months. Our recipe has an added bonus: The cooked chicken
can be used in casseroles and salads. So rich, it serves as a
"base" for many of our other soups and stews.

PREP: 10 MINUTES PLUS COOLING   **COOK:** 4 HOURS 30 MINUTES
MAKES: ABOUT 5½ CUPS

1   chicken (3 to 3½ pounds), including neck (reserve giblets for another use)

2   carrots, peeled and cut into 2-inch pieces

1   stalk celery, cut into 2-inch pieces

1   medium onion, unpeeled and cut into quarters

5   parsley sprigs

1   garlic clove, unpeeled

½   teaspoon dried thyme

½   bay leaf

1 In 6-quart saucepot, combine chicken, chicken neck, carrots, celery, onion, parsley, garlic, thyme, bay leaf, and 3 quarts water or enough water to cover; heat to boiling over high heat. With slotted spoon, skim foam from surface. Reduce heat to low; cover and simmer, turning chicken once and skimming foam occasionally, 1 hour.

2 Remove from heat; transfer chicken to large bowl. When cool enough to handle, remove skin and bones from chicken. (Reserve chicken meat for another use.) Return skin and bones to Dutch oven and heat to boiling over high heat. Skim foam; reduce heat to low and simmer, uncovered, 3 hours.

3 Strain broth through colander into large bowl; discard solids. Strain again though sieve into containers; cool. Cover and refrigerate to use within 3 days, or freeze up to 4 months.

4 To use, skim and discard fat from surface of broth.

EACH CUP: ABOUT 36 CALORIES, 3G PROTEIN, 4G CARBOHYDRATE, 1G TOTAL FAT (1G SATURATED), 0G FIBER, 91MG SODIUM.

Pressure-Cooker
CHICKEN BROTH

In 6-quart pressure cooker, place all ingredients for Chicken Broth but use only 4 cups water. Following manufacturer's directions, cover pressure cooker and bring up to high pressure (15 pounds). Cook 15 minutes. Remove cooker from heat and allow pressure to drop 5 minutes, then follow manufacturer's directions for quick release of pressure. Strain broth through colander into large bowl; discard solids. Strain again through sieve into containers; cool. Meanwhile, remove skin and bones from chicken; discard. (Reserve chicken for another use.) Cover broth and refrigerate to use within 3 days, or freeze up to 4 months. To use, skim and discard fat from surface of broth.

How to Freeze and Reheat Soups

• Cool in containers, uncovered, at least 30 minutes in refrigerator or until warm. Cover containers tightly; label and freeze up to 3 months.

• When ready to serve, place frozen soup, still in covered containers, up to rim in bowl or sink of hot water 1 to 3 minutes or until sides separate from containers. Invert into saucepan or skillet; add ¼ to ½ cup water. Cover and heat to boiling over medium heat, stirring occasionally; boil 1 minute, stirring.

• Or, invert into microwave-safe bowl or baking dish; cover with waxed paper or vented plastic wrap. Heat in microwave oven on Defrost until most ice crystals are gone and mixture can be easily stirred. Then heat on High until mixture reaches 165°F on instant-read thermometer, stirring gently once during heating.

Classic Chicken Noodle
SOUP

You can use the chicken from the Chicken Broth recipe (page 38) and your preferred noodle to make this family classic.

PREP: 15 MINUTES **COOK:** 20 MINUTES
MAKES: 4 MAIN-DISH SERVINGS

6 cups chicken broth or 6 cups Chicken Broth (page 38)

2 stalks celery, chopped

1 medium carrot, chopped

2 cups cooked chicken, shredded

2 cups cooked noodles

2 tablespoons fresh dill, chopped

1 In a 5-quart saucepan, heat chicken broth over medium heat until simmering. Add celery and carrot and cook until tender, about 8 to 10 minutes.

2 Add shredded chicken to soup; heat through. Reduce heat to low and add cooked noodles and dill. Serve and garnish with dill and any leftover celery.

EACH SERVING: ABOUT 251 CALORIES, 23G PROTEIN, 25G CARBOHYDRATE, 5G TOTAL FAT (1G SATURATED), 2G FIBER, 697MG SODIUM.

Lemon-Dill Chicken Meatball
SOUP

This light and satisfying supper is exceptionally good,
and good for you! For photo, see page 36.

PREP: 15 MINUTES   **COOK:** 30 MINUTES
MAKES: 4 MAIN-DISH SERVINGS

2   carrots, sliced

2   stalks celery, sliced

1   small onion, chopped

2   tablespoons olive oil

5   cups lower-sodium chicken broth or 5
    cups Chicken Broth (page 38)

1¾ cups bulgur

12 ounces ground chicken breast

¼   cup fresh dill, finely chopped

1   teaspoon grated lemon zest

Salt

¼   teaspoon ground black pepper

1 In a 6- to 7-quart saucepot over medium heat,
cook carrots, celery, and onion in olive oil for
10 minutes while stirring. Add chicken broth
and 3 cups water; heat to boiling on high. Stir in
bulgur. Reduce heat; simmer 8 to 10 minutes or
until bulgur is almost tender.

2 Meanwhile, combine ground chicken breast,
dill, lemon zest, and ¼ teaspoon each salt and
pepper. Form chicken mixture into 1-inch balls;
add to simmering soup along with ¼ teaspoon
salt. Cook 6 minutes or until cooked through.

EACH SERVING: ABOUT 435 CALORIES, 22G PROTEIN,
53G CARBOHYDRATE, 16G TOTAL FAT (1G SATURATED),
9G FIBER, 925MG SODIUM.

Chicken & DUMPLINGS

For a stick-to-your-ribs supper, nothing beats chicken and dumplings. Our low-sodium, lean-chicken version is rich in flavor but includes only 2 grams of saturated fat and a relatively slim 385 calories. Simmering the skim-milk dumplings in stock makes them as fluffy and delicious as buttery ones and transforms the broth into a silky sauce.

PREP: 30 MINUTES **COOK:** 20 MINUTES
MAKES: 4 MAIN-DISH SERVINGS

1¼ pounds boneless chicken breasts, cut into 1-inch chunks

¾ teaspoon salt

¼ teaspoon ground black pepper

2 tablespoons vegetable oil

4 large carrots, peeled and thinly sliced

3 large stalks celery, thinly sliced

1 onion, chopped

1 can (14½ ounces) lower-sodium chicken broth or 1¾ cups Chicken Broth (page 38)

1 sprig fresh rosemary

½ cup all-purpose flour

½ teaspoon baking soda

2 teaspoons trans-fat-free shortening

¼ cup nonfat milk

1 cup frozen peas

2 tablespoons chopped fresh parsley

1 Heat 6-quart Dutch oven over medium-high heat until hot. Season chicken with ¼ teaspoon each salt and pepper. To pot, add 1 tablespoon oil, then chicken. Cook 2 to 3 minutes or until no longer pink on outside, stirring. Transfer chicken to bowl; reduce heat to medium.

2 To same pot, add remaining 1 tablespoon oil; stir in carrots, celery, and onion. Cook 5 to 7 minutes or until onion is translucent, stirring occasionally. Add broth, rosemary, and 2 cups water; heat to simmering.

3 In small bowl, whisk flour, baking soda, and remaining ½ teaspoon salt. With fork, cut in shortening until mixture forms coarse crumbs. Stir in milk just until dough forms.

4 Stir chicken into simmering broth; cook 2 minutes. Stir in peas; cook 1 minute longer. With slotted spoon, transfer chicken and vegetables to large bowl. Do not remove pot from heat.

5 Drop dough into Dutch oven by teaspoons. Simmer 5 minutes, covered, then uncover and simmer 3 to 5 minutes longer or until dumplings are cooked through.

6 Spoon dumplings and broth over chicken mixture. Divide among bowls and garnish with parsley.

EACH SERVING: ABOUT 385 CALORIES, 39G PROTEIN, 31G CARBOHYDRATE, 11G TOTAL FAT (2G SATURATED), 5G FIBER, 780MG SODIUM.

Southwestern Chicken
SOUP

Classic chicken soup gets a makeover inspired
by spicy Tex-Mex cuisine.

PREP: 15 MINUTES **SLOW COOK:** ABOUT 4 HOURS
MAKES: 6 MAIN-DISH SERVINGS

2   medium russet potatoes, peeled and cut into ½-inch chunks

1   pound skinless, boneless chicken breast halves, cut into quarters

1   pound skinless, boneless chicken thighs, cut into halves

4   cups chicken broth or 4 cups Chicken Broth (page 38)

3   large stalks celery, thinly sliced

1   jalapeño chile, finely chopped

2   teaspoon ground cumin

1   garlic clove, crushed with garlic press

1   teaspoon salt

¼   teaspoon ground black pepper

2   cups frozen corn, thawed

½   cup lightly packed fresh cilantro leaves, finely chopped

1   tablespoon lime juice

1   ripe avocado, chopped

1 In large bowl, combine potatoes and ¼ cup water. Cover with vented plastic wrap and microwave on High 5 minutes or until almost tender. Drain and transfer potatoes to bowl of 7- to 8-quart slow cooker.

2 To same slow-cooker bowl, add chicken, broth, celery, jalapeño, cumin, garlic, salt, and pepper. Replace lid and cook on Low 4 hours or until chicken is cooked through (165°F) but not soft.

3 Transfer chicken to cutting board. Using two forks, pull chicken into bite-size pieces. Return chicken to slow-cooker bowl.

4 Stir corn, cilantro, and lime juice into soup. Divide among serving bowls. Top with avocado.

EACH SERVING: ABOUT 340 CALORIES, 35G PROTEIN, 25G CARBOHYDRATE, 11G TOTAL FAT (2G SATURATED), 5G FIBER, 1,215MG SODIUM.

TIP

Two teaspoons red wine vinegar can be substituted for the lime juice.

Thai Chicken-Basil SOUP

Fresh basil and lime juice give this easy
Thai noodle soup its perky personality.

PREP: 5 MINUTES   **COOK:** 1 HOUR
MAKES: 8 MAIN-DISH SERVINGS

1   tablespoon vegetable oil

1   medium onion, chopped

1   medium poblano chile (3 ounces), seeded
and chopped

4   teaspoons finely chopped, peeled fresh
ginger

3   garlic cloves, thinly sliced

1/4   teaspoon crushed red pepper

3   tablespoons reduced-sodium Asian fish
sauce (see Tip)

2   cartons (32 ounces each) lower-sodium
chicken broth or 8 cups Chicken Broth
(page 38)

1/2   cup packed fresh basil leaves, thinly sliced,
plus basil sprigs for garnish

1½   pounds boneless, skinless chicken thighs,
trimmed of fat, thinly sliced crosswise

1   package (14 ounces) linguine-style
(1/4-inch-wide) rice noodles

3 to 4 large limes

1 In 6-quart Dutch oven, heat oil over medium heat. Add onion and poblano, and cook 10 minutes or until lightly browned and tender, stirring occasionally. Add ginger, garlic, crushed red pepper, and 1 tablespoon fish sauce; cook 1 minute.

2 Add broth, 3 cups water, and half of sliced basil; heat to boiling over high heat. Reduce heat to low; cover and simmer 20 minutes. Uncover; increase heat to medium-high. Stir in chicken and uncooked noodles; heat to boiling. Boil 1 minute.

3 Remove Dutch oven from heat. Skim off fat. Cut 1 lime into wedges and set aside for garnish. Squeeze enough juice from remaining limes to make 1/4 cup. To serve, stir in lime juice, remaining 2 tablespoons fish sauce, and remaining sliced basil. Garnish each serving with basil sprigs. Serve with additional fish sauce and lime wedges.

EACH SERVING: ABOUT 315 CALORIES, 19G PROTEIN, 47G CARBOHYDRATE, 6G TOTAL FAT (1G SATURATED), 1G FIBER, 925MG SODIUM.

TIP

Highly pungent, Asian fish sauce is made from the liquid of salted fermented anchovies. That means a little goes a long way—happily it has an extended shelf life. If you don't have any on hand, substitute half the amount of reduced-sodium soy sauce.

Slow-Cooker Tex-Mex
CHICKEN SOUP

Homemade crispy tortilla strips give this hearty
chicken soup a healthy crunch. For photo, see page 2.

PREP: 20 MINUTES **SLOW COOK:** ABOUT 4 HOURS
MAKES: 6 MAIN-DISH SERVINGS

2½ pounds bone-in, skin-on chicken thighs,
skin removed

4 cups lower-sodium chicken broth or
4 cups Chicken Broth (page 38)

3 large stalks celery, sliced

3 medium carrots, sliced

2 poblano peppers, seeded and chopped

1 medium onion, chopped

3 garlic cloves, chopped

1 tablespoon ground cumin

1 tablespoon ground coriander

2 cans (15 ounces each) white (cannellini)
beans, drained

Salt

8 ounces Monterey Jack cheese, shredded

2 tablespoons lime juice

Chopped avocado, for garnish

Cilantro leaves, for garnish

Sour cream, for garnish

Baked Tortilla Strips, for garnish (optional)

1 To 6- to 7-quart slow-cooker bowl, add chicken,
broth, celery, carrots, peppers, onion, garlic,
cumin, coriander, beans, and ½ teaspoon salt.
Cover and cook on Low 4 to 5 hours or until
carrots are tender.

2 Remove and discard bones from chicken; shred
chicken and return to slow-cooker bowl.

3 Add cheese, lime juice, and ¼ teaspoon salt to
soup in bowl, stirring until cheese melts. Serve
topped with avocado, cilantro, sour cream and
Baked Tortilla Strips, if desired.

4 **Baked Tortilla Strips:** Preheat oven to 425°F.
Stack 4 small corn tortillas; thinly slice into
⅛-inch-wide strips. Arrange in single layer on
large baking sheet. Spray all over with nonstick
cooking spray. Bake 4 to 5 minutes or until deep
golden brown. Let cool completely.

EACH SERVING (SOUP ONLY): ABOUT 445 CALORIES,
40G PROTEIN, 34G CARBOHYDRATE, 16G TOTAL FAT
(7G SATURATED), 14G FIBER, 1,070MG SODIUM.

TIP

To make ahead: Proceed through step 2.
Hold on slow cooker's Keep Warm setting
up to 3 hours or transfer to container and
refrigerate, covered, up to 2 days; reheat
in pot on stove top on medium-high heat,
about 15 minutes or until simmering.
Continue with step 3.

Chicken & Escarole
SOUP WITH MEATBALLS

This soup is sometimes referred to as Italian Wedding Soup,
but it really has nothing to do with weddings.
The "wedding" refers to the "marriage" of its flavors.

PREP: 45 MINUTES **COOK:** 1 HOUR 45 MINUTES
MAKES: 14 FIRST-COURSE SERVINGS

1   chicken (4 pounds), cut into 8 pieces

1   large onion (12 ounces), cut in half

1/4   teaspoon whole black peppercorns

1   bay leaf

1   pound ground meat for meat loaf (beef, pork, and veal)

2   garlic cloves, crushed with garlic press

1   large egg, beaten

1/4   cup chopped fresh parsley

1/2   teaspoon ground black pepper

3/4   cup grated Romano cheese, plus additional for serving

2 3/4 teaspoons salt

1   cup plain dried bread crumbs

    cup milk

1   can (14 to 14 1/2 ounces) chicken broth or 1 3/4 cups Chicken Broth (page 38)

3   carrots, peeled and sliced

2   stalks celery, sliced

1   small head escarole (about 8 ounces), cut into 1/2-inch strips

1 In 8-quart Dutch oven or saucepot, combine chicken, onion, peppercorns, bay leaf, and 12 cups water; heat to boiling over high heat. Reduce heat to low; cover and simmer until chicken is tender, about 1 hour and 15 minutes.

2 Meanwhile, prepare meatballs: In large bowl, combine ground meat, garlic, egg, parsley, pepper, 1/2 cup Romano cheese, and 3/4 teaspoon salt just until well blended but not overmixed. In small bowl, with fork, mix bread crumbs and milk to form thick paste. Mix bread-crumb mixture into meat mixture just until blended. Shape mixture into 1-inch meatballs, handling meat as little as possible, and place 1 inch apart on cookie sheet; cover and refrigerate 30 minutes.

3 Transfer chicken to bowl; set aside until cool enough to handle. Discard skin and bones from chicken; cut chicken into bite-size pieces. Reserve 2 cups cut-up chicken; refrigerate remaining chicken for another use. Strain broth through sieve into large bowl. Skim and discard fat from broth.

4 Return broth to same clean Dutch oven or saucepot. Add broth and 2 teaspoons salt; heat to boiling over high heat. Stir in carrots and celery; heat to boiling. Reduce heat to low; cover and simmer until vegetables are tender, 8 to 10 minutes. Add meatballs and ¼ cup Romano cheese; heat to boiling over high heat. Reduce heat to low; cover and simmer until meatballs are cooked through, about 15 minutes. Stir in escarole and reserved chicken; heat through. Serve with grated Romano cheese.

EACH SERVING: ABOUT 235 CALORIES, 18G PROTEIN, 10G CARBOHYDRATE, 13G TOTAL FAT (5G SATURATED), 2G FIBER, 760MG SODIUM.

Feel Full, Lose Weight

Looking to lose a few pounds? Indulge in soup. Research shows that the best way to start a meal may be with water—or broth-based soup. It fills you up—even more so than other foods low in calorie density. You'll feel full faster and end up eating less at that sitting. Or make soup a meal in itself; with vegetable-based soups, you'll get plenty of fiber to keep you feeling full longer.

Chicken & Bacon
CHOWDER

Smoky bacon and the heat of a little cayenne pepper give
this otherwise traditional chowder a serious kick.

PREP: 15 MINUTES   **COOK:** 30 MINUTES
MAKES: 6 MAIN-DISH SERVINGS

4   slices thick-cut bacon, chopped

3   stalks celery, finely chopped

2   medium shallots, finely chopped

¼   teaspoon ground red pepper (cayenne)

Salt

½   cup all-purpose flour

1   quart lower-sodium chicken broth or 4
    cups Chicken Broth (page 38)

1   pound skinless, boneless chicken thighs

1   pound red potatoes, cut into ½-inch chunks

2   cups whole milk

2   cups fresh or frozen corn

Thinly sliced basil, for garnish

Oyster crackers, for serving

1 In 6-quart saucepot, cook bacon on medium heat until crispy and browned, stirring occasionally. With slotted spoon, transfer to plate; set aside.

2 To pot, add celery, shallots, cayenne, and ¼ teaspoon salt. Cook 7 to 10 minutes or until vegetables are almost tender, stirring occasionally. Sprinkle flour over vegetables. Cook 1 minute, stirring.

3 Slowly stir in broth. Heat to simmering on high heat. Add chicken and potatoes. Reduce heat to medium. Cook 12 to 15 minutes or until chicken is cooked and potatoes are tender, stirring occasionally. With tongs, transfer chicken to bowl and shred. Return chicken to pot. Stir in milk, corn, and ½ teaspoon salt. Cook 3 minutes or until corn is hot. Garnish with basil and reserved bacon. Serve with oyster crackers, if desired.

EACH SERVING: ABOUT 400 CALORIES, 25G PROTEIN, 35G CARBOHYDRATE, 18G TOTAL FAT (9G SATURATED), 3G FIBER, 895MG SODIUM.

Bouillabaisse-Style
CHICKEN SOUP

Instead of a bevy of high-maintenance seafood, this slow-cooker bouillabaisse recipe boasts boneless, skinless chicken thighs simmered in a traditional saffron broth.

PREP: 30 MINUTES   SLOW COOK: ABOUT 8 HOURS ON LOW OR 4 HOURS ON HIGH
MAKES: 8 MAIN-DISH SERVINGS

1   tablespoon olive oil

3   pounds bone-in chicken thighs, skin and fat removed

½   teaspoon salt

¼   teaspoon ground black pepper

1   large bulb fennel (1½ pounds)

½   cup dry white wine

1   onion, chopped

2   garlic cloves, finely chopped

1   can (14½ ounces) chicken broth or 1¾ cups Chicken Broth (page 38)

1   can (14½ ounces) diced tomatoes

1   bay leaf

½   teaspoon dried thyme

¼   teaspoon saffron threads, crumbled

Crusty French bread (optional)

1 In 12-inch skillet, heat oil over medium-high heat until hot. Sprinkle chicken thighs with salt and pepper. Add chicken to skillet in 2 batches and cook, turning once and adding more oil if necessary, until lightly browned on both sides, 7 to 8 minutes per batch. With tongs, transfer chicken to bowl when browned.

2 Meanwhile, trim stems and tough outer layers from fennel bulb. Cut bulb into quarters, then thinly slice crosswise.

3 After chicken is browned, add wine to skillet and heat to boiling, stirring to loosen any browned bits. Boil 1 minute.

4 In 4¼- to 6-quart slow-cooker bowl, combine fennel, onion, garlic, broth, tomatoes with their juice, bay leaf, thyme, and saffron. Top with chicken, any juices in bowl, and wine mixture from skillet; do not stir. Cover slow cooker and cook on Low 8 hours or on High 4 hours.

5 With tongs, transfer chicken to serving bowls. Discard bay leaf. Skim and discard fat from sauce. Pour sauce over chicken. Serve with bread, if you like.

EACH SERVING: ABOUT 175 CALORIES, 22G PROTEIN, 9G CARBOHYDRATE, 6G TOTAL FAT (1G SATURATED), 3KG FIBER, 580MG SODIUM.

Turkey SOUP

What's the Friday after Thanksgiving without turkey soup?
Use your favorite vegetables to personalize this simple recipe.

PREP: 15 MINUTES PLUS OVERNIGHT CHILLING   **COOK:** 5 HOURS
MAKES: 12 FIRST-COURSE SERVINGS

6   carrots, peeled

3   stalks celery

Roasted turkey carcass, plus 2 cups cooked
   turkey meat, finely chopped

2   medium onions, each cut into quarters

5   parsley sprigs

1   garlic clove, peeled

¼   teaspoon dried thyme

½   bay leaf

1¼ teaspoons salt

1   cup regular long-grain rice, cooked as label
   directs

2   tablespoons fresh lemon juice or 1
   tablespoon dry sherry

1 Cut 2 carrots and 1 stalk celery into 2-inch pieces. In 12-quart stockpot, combine turkey carcass, carrot and celery pieces, onions, parsley sprigs, garlic, thyme, bay leaf, and 6 quarts water or enough water to cover; heat to boiling over high heat. Skim foam from surface. Reduce heat and simmer, skimming occasionally, 4 hours.

2 Strain broth through colander set over large bowl; discard solids. Strain again through sieve into several containers; cool. Cover and refrigerate overnight.

3 Remove and discard fat from surface of broth; measure broth and pour into 5-quart saucepot. If necessary, boil broth over high heat until reduced to 10 cups to concentrate flavor.

4 Cut remaining 4 carrots and remaining 2 stalks celery into ½-inch pieces; add to broth with salt. Heat soup to boiling. Reduce heat and simmer until vegetables are tender, about 15 minutes. Stir in cooked rice and turkey; heat through, about 5 minutes. Remove from heat and stir in lemon juice.

EACH SERVING: ABOUT 113 CALORIES, 10G PROTEIN, 12G CARBOHYDRATE, 2G TOTAL FAT (1G SATURATED), 1G FIBER, 355MG SODIUM.

Alphabet SOUP

Filled with veggies and turkey meatballs, this alphabet soup is fit for children and adults alike.

PREP: 18 MINUTES **COOK:** 20 MINUTES
MAKES: 4 MAIN-DISH SERVINGS

8 ounces ground turkey breast

3 tablespoons dried bread crumbs

1 large egg, lightly beaten

¼ teaspoon dried thyme

Salt

½ teaspoon ground black pepper

1 small leek (6 to 8 ounces), white and light green parts only, cut in half and thinly sliced

2 teaspoons vegetable oil

2 stalks celery, finely chopped

4 cups lower-sodium chicken broth or 4 cups Chicken Broth (page 38)

1 can (14½ ounces) no-salt-added diced tomatoes, drained

1 cup fresh corn kernels

4 ounces alphabet pasta

8 ounces small broccoli florets

1 cup frozen peas

1 In medium bowl, combine turkey, bread crumbs, egg, thyme, and ¼ teaspoon each salt and pepper. Cover and refrigerate.

2 Place leek in bowl of cold water; swish to remove any sand. With hands, transfer leek to colander. Repeat several times with fresh water, until sand is removed. Drain.

3 In 5- to 6-quart saucepot, heat oil on medium. Add celery and leek; cook 6 to 7 minutes or until tender, stirring occasionally. Add broth, tomatoes, corn, and 1 cup water. Cover and heat to boiling on high.

4 Using measuring teaspoon, scoop turkey mixture into balls and drop into pot. Stir in pasta, broccoli, peas, and ¼ teaspoon salt. Reduce heat to medium-low and simmer 7 to 9 minutes or until pasta is tender and meatballs are cooked through, stirring occasionally.

EACH SERVING: ABOUT 335 CALORIES, 27G PROTEIN, 47G CARBOHYDRATE, 5G TOTAL FAT (1G SATURATED), 7G FIBER, 885MG SODIUM.

Brown Beef STOCK

For a richer, meatier flavor, use four pounds of beef
bones and one pound of oxtails.

PREP: 5 MINUTES   **COOK:** 7 HOURS 30 MINUTES
MAKES: ABOUT 5 CUPS

5   pounds beef bones, cut into 3-inch pieces

2   medium onions, each cut in half

3   carrots, peeled and cut in half

2   stalks celery, cut in half

1   small bunch parsley

1   bay leaf

½   teaspoon dried thyme

1 Preheat oven to 450°F. Spread beef bones, onions, carrots, and celery in large roasting pan (17½" by 11½"). Roast, stirring every 15 minutes, until well browned, about 1 hour.

2 With tongs, transfer browned bones and vegetables to 6-quart saucepot. Carefully pour off fat from roasting pan. Add 1 cup water to roasting pan and heat to boiling, stirring until browned bits are loosened from bottom of pan; add to pot. Add 12 cups water, parsley, bay leaf, and thyme to pot. Heat to boiling over high heat, skimming foam from surface. Reduce heat and simmer, skimming foam occasionally, 6 hours.

3 Strain broth through colander into large bowl; discard solids. Strain again through fine-mesh sieve into containers. Cool. Cover and refrigerate to use within 3 days, or freeze up to 4 months.

4 To use, skim and discard fat from surface of stock.

EACH CUP: ABOUT 39 CALORIES, 5G PROTEIN,
5G CARBOHYDRATE, 0G TOTAL FAT (0G SATURATED),
0G FIBER, 73MG SODIUM.

Gingery Meatball SOUP

Fresh ginger gives this hearty meatball soup a lively kick of flavor.

PREP: 20 MINUTES **COOK:** 15 MINUTES
MAKES: 6 MAIN-DISH SERVINGS

1   pound ground pork

2   green onions, finely chopped

3   garlic cloves, finely chopped

1   piece (1 inch) peeled fresh ginger, finely chopped

½   teaspoon salt

½   teaspoon ground black pepper

2   quarts lower-sodium chicken broth or 8 cups Chicken Broth (page 38)

8   ounces snow peas, sliced

3   cups cooked white rice

1 Arrange oven rack 6 inches from broiler heat source. Preheat broiler on high. Line large-rimmed baking sheet with foil.

2 In medium bowl, combine pork, green onions, garlic, ginger, salt, and pepper. Form mixture into bite-size meatballs (about 1 inch each); arrange in single layer on prepared baking sheet. Broil 5 to 7 minutes or until browned.

3 Meanwhile, in covered 5-quart saucepot, heat broth to simmering on high heat. Uncover; add snow peas, rice, and broiled meatballs. Reduce heat to medium; simmer 5 minutes or until meatballs are cooked through and snow peas are tender.

EACH SERVING: ABOUT 300 CALORIES, 19G PROTEIN, 26G CARBOHYDRATE, 12G TOTAL FAT (4G SATURATED), 2G FIBER, 835MG SODIUM.

Country Beef & Veggie
SOUP

This is so filling it can almost be considered a stew.
Serve with crusty farmhouse white bread for a cozy Sunday supper.

PREP: 25 MINUTES PLUS SOAKING BEANS   **COOK:** 1 HOUR 45 MINUTES
MAKES: 8 MAIN-DISH SERVINGS

8   ounces dry large lima beans (1½ cups), rinsed and picked through

1   tablespoon vegetable oil

2   pounds beef shank cross cuts, each 1½ inches thick

2   medium onions, finely chopped

3   garlic cloves, minced

⅛   teaspoon ground cloves

4   large carrots, peeled and cut into ½-inch pieces

2   large stalks celery, cut into ½-inch pieces

8   ounces green cabbage (about ½ small head), cored and cut into ½-inch pieces (about 5 cups)

1   can (14 to 14½ ounces) beef broth, or 1¾ cups Brown Beef Stock (page 56)

2   teaspoons salt

½   teaspoon dried thyme leaves

½   teaspoon ground black pepper

3   medium all-purpose potatoes (1 pound), peeled and cut into ¾-inch pieces

1   can (14 to 14½ ounces) diced tomatoes

1   cup frozen whole-kernel corn

1   cup frozen peas

¼   cup chopped fresh parsley

1 In large bowl, place beans and enough water to cover by 2 inches. Soak overnight. (Or, in 4-quart saucepan, heat beans and enough water to cover by 2 inches to boiling over high heat; cook 2 minutes. Remove from heat; cover and let stand 1 hour.) Drain and rinse beans.

2 In 8-quart Dutch oven, heat vegetable oil over medium-high heat until hot. Add half of beef shanks and cook until meat is well browned, using slotted spoon to transfer beef shanks to plate as it is browned. Repeat with remaining beef.

3 Reduce heat to medium; add onions and cook, stirring occasionally, until tender, about 5 minutes. Add garlic and cloves; cook, stirring, 30 seconds. Return beef to Dutch oven. Stir in carrots, celery, cabbage, broth, salt, thyme, pepper, and 4½ cups water; heat to boiling over high heat. Reduce heat to low; cover and simmer until beef is tender, about 1 hour.

4 Meanwhile, in 4-quart saucepan, heat beans and 5 cups water to boiling over high heat. Reduce heat to low; cover and simmer until beans are tender, about 30 minutes. Drain beans.

5 Add potatoes and cooked beans to cooked beef; heat to boiling over high heat. Reduce heat to low; cover and simmer 5 minutes. Stir in tomatoes with their juice; cover and simmer until potatoes are tender, about 10 minutes longer.

6 With slotted spoon, transfer beef shanks to plate; set aside until cool enough to handle. Remove and discard bones and fat; cut beef into ½-inch pieces. Return beef to Dutch oven. Add frozen corn and peas; heat through. To serve, sprinkle with parsley.

....

EACH SERVING: ABOUT 375 CALORIES, 27G PROTEIN, 44G CARBOHYDRATE, 11G TOTAL FAT (4G SATURATED), 10G FIBER, 990MG SODIUM.

TIP

Try this trick if you've oversalted a pot of soup: Peel and quarter a potato and simmer in the soup for 10 to 15 minutes; remove before serving. The potato's starchy texture should absorb the excess salt— unless you really dumped in a lot, in which case you may be stuck with a salty dish.

Clam Chowder (page 67)

3 | Fish & Shellfish

Seafood requires little cooking time but contributes subtle and delicious flavors to dishes, including soups. Many of our recipes use seafood stock made from shrimp or lobster shells. For the best results, add the clams, mussels, shrimp, lobster, or other seafood toward the end of the recipe unless specified. We assure your family and friends will enjoy our robust New England-inspired chowders, delicious Shrimp & Sausage Gumbo, indulgent Lobster Bisque, and other succulent soups in this chapter.

Shrimp BISQUE

Bisque doesn't get any tastier than this. Serve it as an
elegant first course or for lunch with a salad of greens and pears.

PREP: 30 MINUTES   **COOK:** 1 HOUR 10 MINUTES
MAKES: 10 FIRST-COURSE SERVINGS

1   pound medium shrimp

3   tablespoons butter or margarine

2   cans (14 to 14½ ounces each) lower-sodium
     chicken broth or 3½ cups Chicken Broth
     (page 38)

1   cup dry white wine

2   medium carrots, chopped

2   medium stalks celery, chopped

1   large onion (12 ounces), chopped

2   tablespoons regular long-grain rice

1¼   teaspoons salt

¼   to ¼ teaspoon ground red pepper (cayenne)

1   bay leaf

1   can (14 to 14½ ounces) diced tomatoes

1   cup half-and-half

2   tablespoons brandy or dry sherry

Fresh chives, for garnish

1 Shell and devein shrimp; reserve shells.

2 In nonreactive 5-quart Dutch oven, melt
1 tablespoon butter over medium heat. Add
shrimp shells and cook, stirring often, 5 minutes.

3 Add broth, wine, and ½ cup water and heat to
boiling over high heat. Reduce heat to low; cover
and simmer 15 minutes. Strain broth into 4-cup
measuring cup or small bowl, pressing on shells
with back of spoon to extract any remaining
liquid. Discard shells.

4 In same Dutch oven, melt remaining
2 tablespoons butter over medium-high heat. Add
shrimp and cook, stirring occasionally, until they
turn opaque throughout, about 3 minutes. With
slotted spoon, transfer shrimp to another small
bowl.

5 Add carrots, celery, and onion to Dutch oven
and cook, stirring occasionally, until lightly
browned, 10 to 12 minutes.

6 Return broth mixture to Dutch oven. Add rice,
salt, ground red pepper, and bay leaf and heat
to boiling over high heat. Reduce heat to low;
cover and simmer until rice is very tender, about
20 minutes. Add tomatoes with their juice and
cook 10 minutes longer.

7 Remove Dutch oven from heat. Remove and discard bay leaf. Add shrimp.

8 Spoon one-fourth of shrimp mixture into blender; cover, with center part of lid removed to let steam escape, and puree until very smooth. Pour into large bowl. Repeat with each quarter of remaining mixture.

9 Return soup to Dutch oven. Add half-and-half and brandy; heat through over medium heat (do not boil or soup may curdle). Garnish with fresh chives.

EACH SERVING: ABOUT 145 CALORIES, 10G PROTEIN, 9G CARBOHYDRATE, 7G TOTAL FAT (4G SATURATED), 1G FIBER, 739MG SODIUM.

Shrimp Savvy

- You can buy shrimp all year-round—about 95 percent of what's sold in the United States has been previously frozen.

- Depending on variety, shrimp shells can be light gray, brownish pink, or red, but when cooked, all will turn reddish.

- Select raw shrimp with firm-looking meat and shiny shells that feel full. Avoid black spots, which are a sign of aging. The heads are usually removed before shrimp are sold; if not, gently pull the head away from the body before shelling. Cooked, shelled shrimp should be plump with white flesh.

- When buying shrimp in their shells, always buy more than you need to account for the shelled weight. For example, 1¼ pounds shrimp yields 1 pound shelled and deveined.

- Shrimp can be shelled before or after cooking. Though shell-on shrimp can be more flavorful, it's often more convenient to shell before cooking.

- Deveining small and medium shrimp is optional. However, do remove the vein of large shrimp; it can contain grit.

- Although small shrimp are cheaper, they're harder to peel and, pound for pound, may not be as good a value.

- Cook raw shrimp briefly, just until opaque throughout; heat cooked shrimp just until warmed through.

- Allow about ¼ pound of shelled shrimp per serving.

New England Shrimp
CHOWDER

This skinnied-down chowder gets its velvety richness from potatoes and reduced-fat milk—and still delivers plenty of calcium to strengthen bones.

PREP: 15 MINUTES   **COOK:** ABOUT 30 MINUTES
MAKES: 4 MAIN-DISH SERVINGS

2   tablespoons extra virgin olive oil

1   medium onion, coarsely chopped

2   stalks celery, coarsely chopped

1   large russet potato, peeled and cut into ½-inch chunks

1   quart lower-sodium chicken broth or 4 cups Chicken Broth (page 38)

2   (8-ounce) bottles clam juice

2   cups corn kernels

1   teaspoon fresh thyme leaves, plus sprigs for garnish

¼   teaspoon smoked paprika

¼   teaspoon ground black pepper

12   ounces shelled, deveined shrimp, coarsely chopped

1   cup reduced-fat (2%) milk

2   medium tomatoes, seeded and finely chopped

4   whole-grain dinner rolls

1 In 6-quart saucepot, heat oil over medium heat. Add onion, celery, and potato. Cook 5 minutes while stirring. Add broth and clam juice. Heat to boiling on high. Cover partially; boil 10 to 15 minutes or until potato is very tender, stirring often.

2 With hand blender (or in batches in blender), puree mixture until smooth. Add corn, thyme, paprika, and pepper. Heat to simmering over medium heat. Simmer 5 minutes while stirring.

3 To pot, add shrimp and milk. Cook 3 to 5 minutes or until shrimp just turn opaque, stirring occasionally. Divide chowder among 4 bowls. Top each with tomato; garnish with thyme. Serve with whole-grain rolls.

EACH SERVING: ABOUT 425 CALORIES, 23G PROTEIN, 60G CARBOHYDRATE, 12G TOTAL FAT (2G SATURATED), 8G FIBER, 1,440MG SODIUM.

Shrimp & Sausage GUMBO

Just like they make it on the bayou—but easier, with frozen okra and canned broth—this Creole specialty is served with rice. Bake a pan of your favorite corn bread (from a mix or from scratch) to round out the meal.

PREP: 10 MINUTES   **COOK:** 40 MINUTES
MAKES: 6 MAIN-DISH SERVINGS

1   cup regular long-grain rice

1   pound hot Italian-sausage links, casings pierced with a fork

3   tablespoons vegetable oil

¼   cup all-purpose flour

2   medium stalks celery, cut into ¼-inch pieces

1   medium green pepper, cut into ¼-inch pieces

1   medium onion, cut into ¼-inch pieces

1   can (14 to 14½ ounces) chicken broth or 1¾ cups Chicken Broth (page 38)

1   package (10 ounces) frozen whole okra

2   teaspoons hot pepper sauce

¼   teaspoon dried thyme

¼   teaspoon dried oregano

1   bay leaf

1   pound large shrimp, shelled and deveined, with tail part of shell left on

Oregano sprigs (optional)

1 Prepare rice as label directs; keep warm.

2 Heat 5-quart Dutch oven or saucepot over medium-high heat until hot. Add sausages and cook, turning often, until very brown, about 10 minutes. With slotted spoon, transfer sausages to plate to cool slightly. Cut each sausage crosswise into thirds.

3 Discard all but 1 tablespoon drippings from Dutch oven. Add oil and heat over medium heat until hot. Stir in flour until blended and cook, stirring frequently, until flour is dark brown but not burned. Add celery, green pepper, and onion and cook, stirring occasionally, until tender, 8 to 10 minutes.

4 Return sausages to Dutch oven. Gradually stir in chicken broth, okra, hot pepper sauce, thyme, oregano, bay leaf, and ½ cup water; heat to boiling. Reduce heat to low; cover and simmer 15 minutes. Add shrimp and cook, uncovered, until shrimp turn opaque throughout, about 2 minutes. Remove and discard bay leaf.

5 To serve, divide rice equally among 6 bowls and top with gumbo. Garnish with oregano sprigs, if you like.

EACH SERVING: ABOUT 495 CALORIES, 29G PROTEIN, 38G CARBOHYDRATE, 25G TOTAL FAT (7G SATURATED), 2G FIBER, 820MG SODIUM.

Clam CHOWDER

This New England–style soup, chunky with carrots, corn, and potatoes, is as satisfying as any cream-based chowder. Convenient canned clams make it weeknight-doable. For photo, see page 60.

For photo, see page 60.

PREP: 25 MINUTES **COOK:** 1 HOUR 5 MINUTES
MAKES: 4 MAIN-DISH SERVINGS

1	medium celery root (1¼ pounds), peeled
2	large carrots
2	large stalks celery
2	large Yukon gold potatoes, scrubbed
1	large onion
1	tablespoon canola oil
2	sprigs fresh thyme
⅛	teaspoon salt
¼	teaspoon ground black pepper
1	bottle (8 ounces) clam juice
2	tablespoons cornstarch
1	cup reduced-fat (2%) milk
2	cans (10 ounces each) whole baby clams, drained
1	cup fresh or frozen (thawed) corn kernels
¼	cup chopped fresh parsley leaves

1 Cut celery root, carrots, celery, potatoes, and onion into ½-inch chunks. In 6-quart saucepot, heat oil on medium. Stir in chopped vegetables, thyme, salt, and black pepper. Cover; cook 12 minutes or until onion softens, stirring occasionally.

2 Add clam juice and 2 cups water; heat to boiling on high heat. Cover; reduce heat to simmer 20 to 25 minutes or until vegetables are tender, stirring occasionally.

3 In cup, stir cornstarch into milk until dissolved. Add to soup; heat to simmering, stirring. Cook 2 minutes or until thickened, stirring. Add clams and corn; cook 3 minutes or until hot, stirring. Top with parsley.

EACH SERVING: ABOUT 425 CALORIES, 33G PROTEIN, 58G CARBOHYDRATE, 7G TOTAL FAT (2G SATURATED), 7G FIBER, 530MG SODIUM.

Mussel SOUP

Easy and satisfying, this soup is best served with
Italian bread to soak up every last drop.

PREP: 15 MINUTES   **COOK:** 20 MINUTES
MAKES: 4 MAIN-DISH SERVINGS

1   tablespoon olive oil

1   large onion (12 ounces), sliced

2   garlic cloves, minced

1   can (28 ounces) plum tomatoes in puree

1   bottle (8 ounces) clam juice

½   cup dry white wine

¼   teaspoon salt

⅛   teaspoon crushed red pepper

2   pounds small mussels, scrubbed and
    debearded (see Tip)

2   tablespoons chopped fresh parsley

2   green onions, chopped

1 In nonreactive 5-quart Dutch oven, heat oil over
medium heat until hot. Add onion and cook until
tender and lightly browned, about 10 minutes.
Add garlic; cook 2 minutes longer.

2 Stir in tomatoes with their puree, clam juice,
wine, salt, red pepper, and 2 cups water and heat
to boiling over high heat, stirring and breaking
up tomatoes with back of spoon. Boil 3 minutes.

3 Add mussels; heat to boiling. Reduce heat to
low; cover and simmer, stirring occasionally, until
mussels open, about 4 to 5 minutes, transferring
mussels to bowl as they open. Discard any
mussels that have not opened.

4 Just before serving, stir in parsley and spoon
broth over mussels. Garnish with green onions.

EACH SERVING: ABOUT 160 CALORIES, 11G PROTEIN,
16G CARBOHYDRATE, 6G TOTAL FAT (1G SATURATED),
3G FIBER, 790MG SODIUM.

TIP

To clean mussels, scrub them well under
cold running water. Cultivated mussels
usually do not have beards, but if you need
to debeard the mussels, grasp the hairlike
beard with your thumb and forefinger and
pull it away from the shell, or scrape it off
with a knife.

Lobster BISQUE

When you serve lobster, save the shells and cooking liquid and make this splendid soup the next day.

PREP: 15 MINUTES   **COOK:** 1 HOUR 15 MINUTES
MAKES: 4 FIRST-COURSE SERVINGS

2   tablespoons butter or margarine

1   medium onion, chopped

1   carrot, peeled and chopped

1   stalk celery, chopped

1   garlic clove, finely chopped

3   tablespoons tomato paste

Leftover shells and heads from 4 steamed lobsters

2   tablespoons cognac or brandy

2   bottles (8 ounces each) clam juice or 2 cups cooking liquid from steaming lobsters

3   parsley sprigs

1/8   teaspoon dried thyme

Pinch ground nutmeg

Pinch ground red pepper (cayenne)

3   tablespoons all-purpose flour

3/4   cup heavy or whipping cream

1 In 12-quart nonreactive stockpot, melt butter over medium heat. Add onion, carrot, celery, and garlic and cook until onion is tender, about 5 minutes. Stir in tomato paste.

2 Increase heat to high and add lobster shells; cook, stirring occasionally, 5 minutes. Stir in cognac and cook until liquid has evaporated. Add 6 cups water, clam juice, parsley, thyme, nutmeg, and ground red pepper; heat to boiling. Reduce heat; cover and simmer 30 minutes.

3 Strain soup through sieve into 4-quart saucepan; discard solids. Heat to boiling over high heat; boil until reduced to 5 cups, 10 to 15 minutes.

4 In small bowl, with wire whisk, whisk flour into cream until blended and smooth. Gradually whisk cream mixture into soup; heat just to boiling, whisking constantly. Reduce heat and simmer 2 minutes.

EACH SERVING: ABOUT 258 CALORIES, 3G PROTEIN, 12G CARBOHYDRATE, 22G TOTAL FAT (14G SATURATED), 1G FIBER, 44MG SODIUM.

Peruvian Fisherman's
SOUP

A true treat for seafood lovers, this typically Peruvian mixture of shrimp and fish is spiced with chiles and brightened with lime.

PREP: 30 MINUTES   **COOK:** 25 MINUTES
MAKES: 6 MAIN-DISH SERVINGS

1   tablespoon vegetable oil

1   medium onion, finely chopped

2   garlic cloves, minced

2   serrano or jalapeño chiles, seeded and minced

1   pound red potatoes, cut into ¾-inch pieces

3   bottles (8 ounces each) clam juice

¾   teaspoon salt

⅛   teaspoon dried thyme

1   lime

1   pound monkfish, dark membrane removed, cut into 1-inch pieces

1   pound medium shrimp, shelled and deveined, with tail part of shell left on, if you like

¼   cup chopped fresh cilantro

1 In 4-quart saucepan, heat oil over medium heat until hot. Add onion and cook, stirring often, until tender, about 10 minutes. Stir in garlic and serranos and cook 30 seconds. Add potatoes, clam juice, salt, thyme, and 2 cups water; heat to boiling over high heat. Reduce heat to low; simmer 10 minutes.

2 Cut lime in half; cut half into wedges and set aside. Add remaining lime half and monkfish to soup; cover and cook 5 minutes. Stir in shrimp and cook, just until shrimp turn opaque throughout, 3 to 5 minutes longer.

3 Remove lime half; squeeze juice into soup and discard rind. Sprinkle soup with cilantro; serve with lime wedges.

....

EACH SERVING: ABOUT 215 CALORIES, 26G PROTEIN, 16G CARBOHYDRATE, 5G TOTAL FAT (1G SATURATED), 2G FIBER, 640MG SODIUM.

Hearty Fish CHOWDER

Cod, potatoes, and a sprinkling of crumbled bacon make every bite of this creamy chowder rich and satisfying.

PREP: 20 MINUTES **COOK:** 30 MINUTES
MAKES: 4 MAIN-DISH SERVINGS

4   slices center-cut bacon

1   large carrot, peeled and chopped

1   medium celery root (13 ounces), peeled and chopped

1   large all-purpose potato (12 ounces), peeled and chopped

2   small onions (4 to 6 ounces each), chopped

2   tablespoons all-purpose flour

1   cup bottled clam juice

1   pound skinless cod fillets, cut into 1-inch chunks

½   cup reduced-fat (2%) milk

¼   teaspoon salt

⅛   teaspoon ground black pepper

Chopped fresh parsley leaves, for garnish

1 In 6- to 7-quart saucepot, cook bacon over medium heat 5 to 7 minutes or until browned and crisp, turning occasionally. Drain on paper towels; set aside. Discard all but 1 tablespoon bacon fat. Keep saucepot with rendered bacon fat over medium heat.

2 While bacon cooks, in large microwave-safe bowl, combine carrot, celery root, potato, and 2 tablespoons water. Cover with vented plastic wrap and microwave on High 5 minutes or until vegetables are just tender.

3 Add onion to saucepot and cook 6 to 8 minutes or until tender, stirring occasionally. Add carrot mixture and cook 2 minutes, stirring.

4 Add flour and cook 2 minutes, stirring. Add clam juice and ½ cup water and whisk until smooth. Heat to boiling, stirring occasionally. Add cod chunks, cover, and cook 4 to 5 minutes or until fish just turns opaque throughout.

5 Stir in milk, salt, and pepper. Cook 1 to 2 minutes or until hot but not boiling. Spoon chowder into shallow bowls; sprinkle with parsley and crumble 1 strip bacon over each serving.

EACH SERVING: ABOUT 310 CALORIES, 27G PROTEIN, 35G CARBOHYDRATE, 7G TOTAL FAT (3G SATURATED), 5G FIBER, 595MG SODIUM.

ZUPPA de Pesce

This classic Italian fish soup features fresh mussels and chunks of cod in a tomato and white wine broth spiked with fennel seeds and crushed red pepper.

PREP: 20 MINUTES   **COOK:** 20 MINUTES
MAKES: 4 MAIN-DISH SERVINGS

1   tablespoon olive oil

1   small onion, finely chopped

1   small red bell pepper, chopped

1   large garlic clove, crushed with garlic press

½   teaspoon fennel seeds

⅛   teaspoon crushed red pepper

¾   cup dry white wine

1   can (28 ounces) whole tomatoes in juice, coarsely chopped

½   teaspoon salt

12 ounces cod or Alaskan pollock fillet, cut into 2-inch pieces

1   pound mussels, scrubbed and beards removed (see Tip on page 68)

8   ounces medium shrimp, shelled and deveined

½   cup fresh basil leaves, julienned

1 In 5- to 6-quart Dutch oven over medium, heat oil. Add onion and chopped red bell pepper; cook 6 to 8 minutes or until tender. Add garlic, fennel, and crushed red pepper; cook 1 minute longer, stirring. Add wine; heat to boiling.

2 Stir in tomatoes with their juice, 1 cup water, and salt; heat to boiling. Add cod, mussels, and shrimp; heat to boiling. Reduce heat to low; cover. Simmer 8 to 9 minutes or until cod and shrimp turn opaque and mussels open. Discard any unopened mussels. To serve, sprinkle with basil leaves.

EACH SERVING: ABOUT 265 CALORIES, 37G PROTEIN, 15G CARBOHYDRATE, 6G TOTAL FAT (1G SATURATED), 3G FIBER, 805MG SODIUM.

*Roasted Chicken & Mushroom
Ramen Bowl (page 84)*

4 | Noodle & Bean

Noodles and beans are great ingredients that supplement a bowl of broth. No matter the shape—from long Asian noodles like in our Roasted Chicken & Mushroom Ramen Bowl, to Italian pastas such as macaroni in our Macaroni, Cabbage & Bean Soup—noodles will always be a crowd favorite. Mild yet creamy beans add body as in our Tuscan Pinto Bean Soup. Our Curried Sweet-Potato & Lentil Soup also packs a mighty punch. Serve these soups as a starter at a dinner party or as a hearty meal to your family.

Pasta e Fagioli WITH SAUSAGE

Pasta e fagioli, Italian pasta and bean soup, becomes a meal-in-a-pot with the addition of sweet sausage and fresh spinach. Using canned beans speeds up cooking.

PREP: 15 MINUTES   **COOK:** 1 HOUR
MAKES: 8 MAIN-DISH SERVINGS

- 1 pound sweet Italian-sausage links, casings removed
- 1 tablespoon olive oil
- 2 medium onions, chopped
- 2 garlic cloves, crushed with garlic press
- 1 can (28 ounces) plum tomatoes
- 2 cans (14½ ounces each) chicken broth or 3½ cups Chicken Broth (page 38)
- 3 cans (15 to 19 ounces) Great Northern or white kidney (cannellini) beans, rinsed and drained
- 6 ounces ditalini or tubetti pasta (1 rounded cup)
- 5 ounces spinach, washed and dried very well, tough stems trimmed, and leaves cut into 1-inch-wide strips

Freshly grated Parmesan cheese (optional)

1 Heat nonreactive 5-quart Dutch oven over medium-high heat until very hot. Add sausage and cook until well browned, breaking up sausage with side of spoon. Transfer sausage to bowl.

2 Reduce heat to medium; add oil to Dutch oven. Add onions and cook until tender and golden, about 10 minutes. Add garlic; cook 1 minute. Add tomatoes with their juice, breaking them up with side of spoon.

3 Add broth and 2 cups water; heat to boiling over high heat. Reduce heat; cover and simmer 15 minutes. Add beans and heat to boiling; cover and simmer 15 minutes longer. Add sausage and heat through.

4 Meanwhile, in 4-quart saucepan, cook pasta as label directs, but do not add salt to water; drain.

5 Just before serving, stir spinach and cooked pasta into soup. Serve with Parmesan, if you like.

EACH SERVING: ABOUT 558 CALORIES, 28G PROTEIN, 65G CARBOHYDRATE, 22G TOTAL FAT (7G SATURATED), 12G FIBER, 1,432MG SODIUM.

Tomato, Escarole &
TORTELLINI SOUP

Perfect weeknight fare. You can use a bag of baby spinach
instead of escarole, if you like.

PREP: 10 MINUTES   **COOK:** 10 MINUTES
MAKES: 4 MAIN-DISH SERVINGS

1   package (8 ounces) frozen or 1 package (9 ounces) fresh tortellini or mini ravioli

2   teaspoons olive oil

2   stalks celery, thinly sliced

1/2   medium head escarole, cut into bite-size pieces (about 5 cups)

1   can (14 to 14½ ounces) diced tomatoes with sweet onions

1   can (14 to 14½ ounces) chicken or vegetable broth, or 1¾ cups Chicken Broth (page 38) or Vegetable Broth (page 14)

1/4   cup freshly grated Romano cheese

1 Cook pasta as label directs.

2 Meanwhile, in 4-quart saucepan, heat oil over medium heat until hot. Add celery and cook, stirring occasionally, until tender-crisp, 5 minutes. Stir in escarole, tomatoes, broth, and 1 cup water. Cover and heat to boiling over high heat. Remove saucepan from heat.

3 Drain tortellini; gently stir into broth mixture. Divide soup equally among 4 large bowls; sprinkle each serving with 1 tablespoon grated Romano.

EACH SERVING: ABOUT 200 CALORIES, 10G PROTEIN, 25G CARBOHYDRATE, 7G TOTAL FAT (3G SATURATED), 5G FIBER, 1,185MG SODIUM.

PASTA E **Piselli**

One fast soup—just 10 minutes to prepare, 15 minutes to cook. Cousin to the Italian favorite Pasta e Fagioli (see page 78), this is made with peas instead. Dust with freshly grated Parmesan or Pecorino Romano for an irresistible touch.

PREP: 10 MINUTES **COOK:** 15 MINUTES
MAKES: 5 MAIN-DISH SERVINGS

2   cups mixed pasta, such as penne, bow tie, or elbow macaroni (about 8 ounces)

2   tablespoons olive oil

3   garlic cloves, crushed with side of chef's knife

2   cans (14 to 14½ ounces each) chicken broth or 3½ cups Chicken Broth (page 38)

1   can (14 to 14½ ounces) diced tomatoes

¼   cup packed fresh basil, coarsely chopped

1   package (10 ounces) frozen peas, thawed

Freshly grated Parmesan or Pecorino Romano cheese

1 Cook pasta as label directs.

2 Meanwhile, in nonreactive 4-quart saucepan, heat oil over medium heat until hot. Add garlic; cook until golden, about 5 minutes.

3 Remove saucepan from heat, then carefully add broth, tomatoes with their juice, basil, and ½ cup water. Return to heat; heat to boiling. Reduce heat to low; cover and simmer 5 minutes. Remove and discard garlic.

4 Stir in peas and pasta; heat through. Serve with Parmesan.

EACH SERVING: ABOUT 400 CALORIES, 11G PROTEIN, 46G CARBOHYDRATE, 7G TOTAL FAT (1G SATURATED), 5G FIBER, 705MG SODIUM.

TIP

In season, use fresh peas (*piselli*). Cook them in the broth until tender before adding the pasta.

SPRING SOUP WITH
Noodles, Ham & Asparagus

Using ramen noodle-soup mix and sliced ham from the deli keeps preparation to a bare minimum—perfect for an impromptu family meal.

PREP: 10 MINUTES **COOK:** 15 MINUTES
MAKES: 4 MAIN-DISH SERVINGS

2   teaspoons vegetable oil

1   large red bell pepper, thinly sliced

1   pound asparagus, trimmed and cut diagonally into 2-inch pieces

4   ounces sliced deli baked ham, cut into ½-inch-wide strips

2   packages (3 ounces each) chicken-flavored ramen noodle-soup mix

2   teaspoons Asian sesame oil

1 In 4-quart saucepan, heat 7 cups water to boiling over high heat.

2 Meanwhile, in nonstick 12-inch skillet, heat oil over medium-high heat until hot. Add red pepper and asparagus and cook until vegetables are tender-crisp, about 7 minutes. Stir in ham and cook until ham is heated through, about 1 minute.

3 Stir ramen noodles with their seasoning packets into boiling water; boil until noodles are tender, about 2 minutes. Remove from heat; stir in ham mixture and sesame oil.

EACH SERVING: ABOUT 300 CALORIES, 12G PROTEIN, 31G CARBOHYDRATE, 15G TOTAL FAT (5G SATURATED), 3G FIBER, 1,205MG SODIUM.

Vegetable Soup
WITH BOW TIES & DILL

Chicken broth brimming with sautéed vegetables and tiny pasta is seasoned with a hint of lemon and lots of fresh dill—a perfect beginning to a light feast!

PREP: 25 MINUTES **COOK:** ABOUT 30 MINUTES
MAKES: 8 FIRST-COURSE SERVINGS

1	lemon
1	tablespoon olive oil
1	large shallot, finely chopped
4	medium carrots, cut lengthwise into quarters, then thinly sliced crosswise
2	medium stalks celery, thinly sliced

About 3½ cans (14 to 14½ ounces each) fat-free chicken broth or 6 cups Chicken Broth (page 38)

1	package (10 ounces) frozen peas
3/4	cup small bow-tie pasta, cooked as label directs
3	tablespoons chopped dill
1/8	teaspoon ground black pepper

1 With vegetable peeler or small knife, remove 3" by 1" strip peel from lemon; squeeze 1 tablespoon juice.

2 In nonstick 5- to 6-quart saucepot, heat oil over medium-high heat until hot. Add shallot and cook, stirring frequently, until golden, about 2 minutes. Add carrots and celery and cook, stirring occasionally, until tender-crisp, 5 minutes.

3 Add broth, lemon peel, and 1 cup water to saucepot; heat to boiling over medium-high heat. Reduce heat to low; cover and simmer until vegetables are tender, about 10 minutes.

4 Remove cover; stir in frozen peas and cook 1 minute longer. Stir in cooked pasta, dill, pepper, and lemon juice; heat through.

EACH SERVING: ABOUT 120 CALORIES, 5G PROTEIN, 17G CARBOHYDRATE, 2G TOTAL FAT (1G SATURATED), 3G FIBER, 770MG SODIUM.

ROASTED CHICKEN & MUSHROOM
Ramen Bowl

Forget everything you know about that 99¢ ramen from college!
The one-bowl meal has gotten an upgrade: It's fancy and delicious,
and you can make it healthy at home. For photo, see page 76.

PREP: 10 MINUTES   **COOK:** 20 MINUTES
MAKES: 4 MAIN-DISH SERVINGS

4   boneless, skinless chicken thighs

2   tablespoons brown sugar

2   tablespoons soy sauce

2   quarts lower-sodium chicken broth or 8
    cups Chicken Broth (page 38)

1   piece (1 inch) fresh ginger, peeled and cut
    into matchsticks

12 ounces ramen noodles

6   ounces spinach

4   ounces shiitake mushrooms, sliced

1   tablespoon Asian sesame oil

Sliced green onions, for garnish

1 Preheat broiler with oven rack 6 inches from
heat source.

2 Toss chicken thighs with brown sugar and soy
sauce; place on a foil-lined baking sheet. Broil for
8 to 10 minutes or until cooked through, turning
once.

3 In 4-quart saucepot, heat chicken broth and
ginger; bring to a boil. Add ramen noodles and
cook. During the last 2 minutes of cooking, stir
in spinach, mushrooms, and sesame oil; cook for
3 minutes.

4 Divide among 4 serving bowls. Top with sliced
broiled chicken and green onions.

....

EACH SERVING: ABOUT 600 CALORIES, 41G PROTEIN,
80G CARBOHYDRATE, 14G TOTAL FAT (3G SATURATED),
5G FIBER, 915MG SODIUM.

TIP

Up your veggie intake: Add a big handful of
shredded carrots to the steamy broth.

Vietnamese Noodle
SOUP

This Asian-style broth is chock-full of delicate rice noodles, fresh snow peas, shiitake mushrooms, and pungent herbs. Called *pho* (pronounced FUH) in Vietnamese, it is named for the wide rice noodles it contains.

PREP: 20 MINUTES **COOK:** 25 MINUTES
MAKES: 4 MAIN-DISH SERVINGS

1 large lime

4 ounces dried flat rice noodles (about ¼ inch wide)

2 cans (14 to 14½ ounces each) chicken broth or vegetable broth, or 3½ cups Chicken Broth (page 38) or Vegetable Broth (page 14)

1 small bunch fresh basil

2 garlic cloves, crushed with side of chef's knife

1 piece (2 inches) peeled fresh ginger, thinly sliced

¼ pound shiitake mushrooms, stems removed and caps thinly sliced

4 ounces snow peas, strings removed and each pod cut diagonally in half

1 tablespoon soy sauce

1 cup loosely packed fresh cilantro, chopped

1 Remove peel from lime with vegetable peeler and reserve; squeeze 1 tablespoon juice.

2 In large bowl, pour enough boiling water over rice noodles to cover; let soak until softened, 7 to 10 minutes.

3 Meanwhile, in 3-quart saucepan, heat broth, basil, garlic, ginger, lime peel, and 2 cups water to boiling over high heat. Reduce heat to low; cover and simmer 10 minutes. Strain broth through sieve set over medium bowl, pressing with back of spoon to extract any remaining liquid; discard solids. Return broth to saucepan.

4 Drain noodles; rinse under cold running water and drain again. Stir mushrooms, snow peas, soy sauce, and noodles into broth mixture; heat to boiling over high heat. Reduce heat to low; cover and simmer 3 minutes. Stir in cilantro and lime juice just before serving.

EACH SERVING: ABOUT 155 CALORIES, 5G PROTEIN, 30G CARBOHYDRATE, 2G TOTAL FAT (1G SATURATED), 2G FIBER, 1,120MG SODIUM.

Miso Spinach NOODLES

Miso paste gives this simple ramen recipe a serious umami boost.

PREP: 10 MINUTES   **COOK:** 15 MINUTES
MAKES: 4 MAIN-DISH SERVINGS

1   teaspoon sugar

½   cup miso paste

4   ounces thin rice noodles

5   ounces baby spinach

1   pound silken or soft tofu, cut into small
    cubes

2   teaspoons sesame oil

2   hard-cooked eggs, halved

1 In a 4-quart saucepot, heat 8 cups water and sugar to boiling on high. Reduce heat to medium.
2 In medium bowl, whisk miso paste and 1 cup boiling water from pot until smooth. To pot, add rice noodles; cook until tender, stirring. Add baby spinach, tofu, sesame oil, and miso mixture, stirring until spinach wilts. Serve with egg halves.

EACH SERVING: ABOUT 330 CALORIES, 17G PROTEIN, 38G CARBOHYDRATE, 13G TOTAL FAT (3G SATURATED), 3G FIBER, 1,375MG SODIUM.

TIP

Looking to branch out with miso? Try it in a chicken marinade (blend 2 tablespoons miso paste with maple syrup and orange juice), salmon glaze (whisk 2 tablespoons with brown sugar and balsamic vinegar), or as a dynamite dressing (mix 1 tablespoon with sherry vinegar, cilantro, and olive oil).

Thai Coconut Soup
WITH BEAN-THREAD NOODLES

This exotic-tasting soup is easy to whip up for a light supper.
Our version uses chicken—or try it with tofu.

PREP: 25 MINUTES **COOK:** 20 MINUTES
MAKES: 4 MAIN-DISH SERVINGS

4 ounces bean-thread noodles (also called saifun, cellophane, or glass noodles)

1 can (14 ounces) light unsweetened coconut milk (not cream of coconut), well stirred

2 garlic cloves, crushed with garlic press

1 tablespoon minced, peeled fresh ginger

½ teaspoon ground coriander

½ teaspoon ground cumin

¼ teaspoon ground red pepper (cayenne)

3 small skinless, boneless chicken-breast halves (12 ounces), thinly sliced, or 1 package (1 pound) firm tofu, rinsed, drained, and cut into 1-inch cubes

2 cans (14 to 14½ ounces each) lower-sodium chicken broth or vegetable broth, or 3½ cups Chicken Broth (page 38) or Vegetable Broth (page 14)

2 green onions, thinly sliced

2 small carrots, cut into 2" by ¼" matchstick strips

½ medium red bell pepper, cut into 2" by ¼" matchstick strips

1 tablespoon Asian fish sauce

2 tablespoons fresh lime juice

1 cup loosely packed fresh cilantro, chopped

1 In large saucepot, heat 3 quarts water to boiling over high heat; remove saucepot from heat. Place noodles in water; soak just until transparent (do not oversoak), 10 to 15 minutes.

2 Meanwhile, in 5-quart Dutch oven, heat ½ cup coconut milk to boiling over medium heat. Add garlic, ginger, coriander, cumin, and ground red pepper and cook, stirring, 1 minute. Increase heat to medium-high; add chicken and cook, stirring constantly, just until chicken loses its pink color throughout. (If using tofu, add with remaining coconut milk in step 4.)

3 Drain noodles. Rinse with cold running water and drain again. With kitchen shears, cut noodles into shorter lengths.

4 To mixture in Dutch oven, add broth, green onions, carrots, red bell pepper, fish sauce, 1 cup water, remaining coconut milk, and tofu, if using, and the cooked noodles; heat just to simmering over medium-high heat, stirring occasionally. Stir in lime juice and cilantro just before serving.

EACH SERVING: ABOUT 340 CALORIES, 25G PROTEIN, 34G CARBOHYDRATE, 11G TOTAL FAT (6G SATURATED), 2G FIBER, 525MG SODIUM.

The Joy of Asian Noodles

Noodle soup started out as a peasant food in China; workers visited noodle shops for filling, inexpensive meals. Today, noodle houses are big business in many parts of Asia. Each type of soup traditionally uses one type of noodle, but any of the noodles listed here can be substituted for one another. These are available in Asian markets, specialty stores, and some supermarkets. (All noodles are dried unless otherwise noted.)

- **Bean-Thread (or Cellophane) Noodles:** made from mung bean starch; they become translucent when cooked.

- **Instant (or Ramen) Noodles:** made from wheat flour; precooked (usually fried); need just a quick boil.

- **Rice Noodles:** made from rice flour; also called rice sticks or rice vermicelli; must soak 20 to 60 minutes before using. (Fresh rice noodles, *sha he fen*, are available in flat sheets that can be cut to desired size.)

- **Te'uchi:** fresh; made from wheat flour; similar to lo mein (below), but handmade, so more expensive.

- **Wheat Flour Noodles:** usually fresh, sometimes dried; called lo mein in Chinese; somen or soba (buckwheat) in Japanese. Somen are sometimes colored green (with green-tea powder), yellow (with egg), or pink (with Japanese red basil oil).

Macaroni, Cabbage
& BEAN SOUP

Rich in fiber and protein, this light yet chunky vegetable soup is ready in less than half an hour.

PREP: 5 MINUTES   **COOK:** 15 MINUTES
MAKES: 6 MAIN-DISH SERVINGS

1½ cups elbow macaroni or mini penne pasta

1   tablespoon olive oil

1   medium onion, cut in half and thinly sliced

½   small head savoy cabbage (about 1 pound), thinly sliced

2   garlic cloves, crushed with garlic press

¼   teaspoon ground black pepper

3   cans (14 to 14½ ounces each) chicken broth or 5¼ cups Chicken Broth (page 38)

2   cans (15 to 19 ounces each) white kidney beans (cannellini), rinsed and drained

Freshly grated Parmesan or Pecorino Romano cheese (optional)

1 Cook macaroni as label directs.

2 Meanwhile, in 5- to 6-quart saucepot, heat oil over medium-high heat until hot. Add onion, cabbage, garlic, and pepper; cook, stirring often, until cabbage begins to wilt, 6 to 8 minutes. Stir in broth, beans, and 1½ cups water; heat to boiling.

3 Meanwhile, drain macaroni. Stir macaroni into cabbage mixture; heat through. Serve with Parmesan, if you like.

....

EACH SERVING: ABOUT 310 CALORIES, 14G PROTEIN, 52G CARBOHYDRATE, 5G TOTAL FAT (1G SATURATED), 15G FIBER, 1,170MG SODIUM.

Hearty
MINESTRONE

Your guests will welcome a steaming bowl of this vegetable-bean soup on a cold winter night. It tastes even better reheated, so it's a good choice to prepare in advance.

PREP: 45 MINUTES **COOK:** 30 MINUTES
MAKES: 10 MAIN-DISH SERVINGS

- 2 slices bacon, chopped
- 2 medium carrots, peeled and cut into ¼-inch pieces
- 1 medium onion, cut into ¼-inch pieces
- 1 large stalk celery, cut into ¼-inch pieces
- 2 garlic cloves, minced
- 3 medium all-purpose potatoes (about 1 pound), peeled and cut into ¼-inch pieces
- 1 can (14 to 14½ ounces) chicken broth or 1¾ cups Chicken Broth (page 38)
- 1 ¼ teaspoons salt
- ¼ teaspoon ground black pepper
- ¼ teaspoon dried thyme
- 1 can (15½ to 19 ounces) white kidney beans (cannellini), rinsed and drained
- ½ pound green beans, trimmed and cut into 1-inch pieces
- ⅓ cup small pasta, such as cavatelli, tubettini, or ditalini
- 1 pound Swiss chard, tough stems trimmed and leaves chopped
- ½ pound spinach, tough stems trimmed
- ½ teaspoon freshly grated lemon peel

Grated Parmesan or Pecorino Romano cheese (optional)

1 In 6-quart saucepot, cook bacon over medium heat until browned. With slotted spoon, transfer bacon to paper towels to drain; set aside.

2 To drippings in saucepot, add carrots, onion, and celery and cook, stirring occasionally, until vegetables are browned, about 15 minutes. Add garlic and cook 30 seconds longer.

3 Add potatoes, broth, salt, pepper, thyme, and 6 cups water; heat to boiling over high heat. Reduce heat to low; cover and simmer 10 minutes.

4 Add white beans, green beans, and pasta; cook 7 minutes longer. Stir in Swiss chard, spinach, and lemon peel; cook until greens are wilted and tender, about 5 minutes longer. Stir in bacon. Serve with grated Parmesan, if you like.

EACH SERVING: ABOUT 370 CALORIES, 5G PROTEIN, 17G CARBOHYDRATE, 2G TOTAL FAT (1G SATURATED), 7G FIBER, 440MG SODIUM.

Split Pea Soup
WITH HAM

On a wintry day, nothing satisfies more than an old-fashioned favorite like split pea soup.

PREP: 10 MINUTES   **COOK:** 1 HOUR 15 MINUTES
MAKES: 6 MAIN-DISH SERVINGS

- 2 tablespoons vegetable oil
- 2 white turnips (6 ounces each), peeled and chopped (optional)
- 2 medium carrots, peeled and finely chopped
- 2 stalks celery, finely chopped
- 1 medium onion, finely chopped
- 1 package (16 ounces) split peas, rinsed and picked through
- 2 smoked ham hocks (1½ pounds)
- 1 bay leaf
- 1 teaspoon salt
- ¼ teaspoon ground allspice

1 In 5-quart Dutch oven, heat oil over medium-high heat until hot. Add turnips, if using, carrots, celery, and onion; cook, stirring frequently, until carrots are tender-crisp, about 10 minutes. Add split peas, ham hocks, 8 cups water, bay leaf, salt, and allspice; heat to boiling over high heat. Reduce heat; cover and simmer 45 minutes.
2 Remove and discard bay leaf. Transfer ham hocks to cutting board; discard skin and bones. Finely chop meat. Return meat to soup; heat through.

EACH SERVING: ABOUT 343 CALORIES, 21G PROTEIN, 52G CARBOHYDRATE, 7G TOTAL FAT (1G SATURATED), 17G FIBER, 1,174MG SODIUM.

Tuscan Pinto
BEAN SOUP

Mild, creamy pinto beans make a great addition to this classic Italian soup made with vibrant greens and savory Parmesan.

PREP: 5 MINUTES **COOK:** 16 MINUTES
MAKES: 4 MAIN-DISH SERVINGS

2 medium stalks celery

1 medium carrot

1 medium onion

1 tablespoon olive oil

2 garlic cloves, crushed with garlic press

3 cups vegetable broth or 3 cups Vegetable Broth (page 14)

2 cans pinto beans

½ pound escarole, chopped

1 cup Parmesan cheese

1 Pulse celery, 1 carrot, and onion, all quartered, in food processor until finely chopped.

2 Heat olive oil in medium saucepot on medium-high heat. Add vegetable mixture and cook, stirring occasionally, 5 minutes or until soft. Add garlic and cook 1 minute. Stir in vegetable broth, beans, and escarole. Bring to a simmer; cook 10 minutes or until escarole wilts.

3 Stir grated Parmesan cheese into soup; divide among 4 bowls. Top with more Parmesan, if desired. Serve with toasted bread slices.

EACH SERVING: ABOUT 330 CALORIES, 19G PROTEIN, 41G CARBOHYDRATE, 11G TOTAL FAT (4G SATURATED), 3G FIBER, 1,365MG SODIUM.

Do Dry Beans Need to Be Soaked?

It's common knowledge that soaking dry beans for hours before using shortens cooking time and improves texture, appearance, and even digestibility. But now some chefs are claiming soaking time can be reduced—even skipped. We tested the old-fashioned method against two shortcuts in the *Good Housekeeping* kitchens, using three batches of black beans and three of Great Northern beans, which were then cooked until tender. The results:

- **The Winner Is . . .** Overnight Soaking. Grandma was right. For the best texture (not too hard or mushy) and appearance (beans held their shape, with practically no split skins), letting beans sit in a bowl of cool tap water until morning really works. Cooking time ranged from 1 hour and 10 minutes to 1 hour and 20 minutes.

- **Second Place:** No Soaking. This method yielded the second most tender and shapely beans, though it required the longest cooking time (1 hour and 35 minutes). But if beans pose digestive problems for you, it's probably better to soak them and discard the water, which helps remove the complex sugars that can cause bloating and gas.

- **Third Place:** Quick Soaking. Bringing the beans to a boil for 2 minutes and then allowing them to soak for an hour in the same water before cooking yielded the most broken beans but definitely the fastest cooking time (1 hour). If you're making a bean soup or chili, where perfect-looking beans don't matter, this method is fine, but we don't recommend it for a bean salad.

- **Note:** Whichever option you choose, remember that cooking time will vary depending on the age/dryness of the beans.

Black-Bean
SOUP

This shortcut soup packs a genuine Tex-Mex wallop of flavor.

PREP: 10 MINUTES   **COOK:** 20 MINUTES
MAKES: 4 MAIN-DISH SERVINGS

1   tablespoon vegetable oil

1   medium onion, finely chopped

2   garlic cloves, crushed with garlic press

2   teaspoons chili powder

1   teaspoon ground cumin

¼   teaspoon crushed red pepper

2   cans (15 to 19 ounces each) black beans, rinsed and drained

1   can (14 to 14½ ounces) chicken broth or 1 ¾ cups Chicken Broth (page 38)

½   cup loosely packed fresh cilantro, chopped

Lime wedges

1 In 3-quart saucepan, heat oil over medium heat until hot. Add onion and cook until tender, about 5 minutes. Stir in garlic, chili powder, cumin, and crushed red pepper; cook 30 seconds. Stir in beans, broth, and 2 cups water; heat to boiling over high heat. Reduce heat to low; simmer, uncovered, 15 minutes.

2 Spoon half of mixture into blender; cover, with center part of cover removed to let steam escape, and puree until almost smooth. Pour into medium bowl. Repear with remaining mixture.

3 Return soup to same saucepan; heat through. Sprinkle with cilantro and serve with lime wedges.

EACH SERVING: ABOUT 265 CALORIES, 22G PROTEIN, 46G CARBOHYDRATE, 6G TOTAL FAT (1G SATURATED), 14G FIBER, 965MG SODIUM.

Red Lentil & Vegetable
SOUP

This meal-in-a-bowl brims with fill-you-up soluble fiber, thanks to the lentils. Soluble fiber helps keep weight down and also helps lower total and "bad" LDL cholesterol. The lentils, spinach, and tomatoes, all rich in potassium, work to keep blood pressure in check, too.

PREP: 10 MINUTES   **COOK:** 20 MINUTES
MAKES: 4 MAIN-DISH SERVINGS

1   tablespoon olive oil

4   medium carrots, chopped

1   small onion, chopped

1   teaspoon ground cumin

1   can (14½ ounces) diced tomatoes

1   can (14 to 14½ ounces) vegetable broth or 1¾ cups Vegetable Broth (page 14)

¼   teaspoon salt

⅛   teaspoon ground black pepper

1   cup dried red lentils

1   bag (5 ounces) baby spinach

1 In 4-quart saucepan, heat oil on medium until hot. Add carrots and onion, and cook 6 to 8 minutes or until lightly browned and tender. Stir in cumin ; cook 1 minute.

2 Add tomatoes, broth, lentils, 2 cups water, salt, and pepper; cover and heat to boiling on high. Reduce heat to low and simmer, covered, 8 to 10 minutes or until lentils are tender. Stir in spinach.

EACH SERVING: ABOUT 265 CALORIES, 16G PROTEIN, 41G CARBOHYDRATE, 5G TOTAL FAT (1G SATURATED), 13G FIBER, 645MG SODIUM.

Curried Sweet-Potato
& LENTIL SOUP

This thick and hearty soup is packed with spicy flavor. Get it going, then call a friend or spend some time with the kids while it simmers.

PREP: 15 MINUTES   **COOK:** ABOUT 1 HOUR 15 MINUTES
MAKES: 8 MAIN-DISH SERVINGS

2   tablespoons butter or margarine

2   medium sweet potatoes (about 12 ounces each), peeled and cut into ½-inch chunks

2   large stalks celery, cut into ¼-inch pieces

1   large onion (12 ounces), cut into ¼-inch pieces

1   garlic clove, minced

1   tablespoon curry powder

1   tablespoon grated, peeled fresh ginger

1   teaspoon ground cumin

1   teaspoon ground coriander

1   teaspoon salt

⅛   teaspoon ground red pepper (cayenne)

2   cans (14½ ounces each) vegetable broth or 3½ cups Vegetable Broth (page 14)

1   package (16 ounces) dry lentils, rinsed and picked through

6   cups water

Yogurt, toasted coconut, and lime wedges (optional)

1 In 6-quart Dutch oven, melt butter over medium heat. Add the sweet potatoes, celery, and onion and cook, stirring occasionally, until onion is tender, about 10 minutes. Add garlic, curry powder, ginger, cumin, coriander, salt, and ground red pepper; cook, stirring, 1 minute.

2 To vegetables in Dutch oven, add broth, lentils, and 6 cups water; heat to boiling over high heat. Reduce heat to low; cover and simmer, stirring occasionally, until lentils are tender, 40 to 45 minutes. Serve with yogurt, toasted coconut, and lime wedges, if you like.

EACH SERVING (WITHOUT YOGURT, COCONUT, AND LIME): ABOUT 295 CALORIES, 15G PROTEIN, 15G CARBOHYDRATE, 5G TOTAL FAT (2G SATURATED), 19G FIBER, 656MG SODIUM.

German Lentil
SOUP

German cooks like to add a meaty ham hock and some chopped bacon to their lentil soups to lend a smoky note.

PREP: 25 MINUTES **COOK:** 1 HOUR 20 MINUTES
MAKES: 6 MAIN-DISH SERVINGS

- 4 slices bacon, cut into ½-inch pieces
- 2 medium onions, chopped
- 2 carrots, peeled and chopped
- 1 large stalk celery, chopped
- 1 package (16 ounces) lentils, rinsed and picked through
- 1 smoked ham hock (1 pound)
- 1 bay leaf
- 1 teaspoon salt
- ½ teaspoon dried thyme
- ½ teaspoon ground black pepper
- 2 tablespoons fresh lemon juice

1 In 5-quart Dutch oven, cook bacon over medium-low heat until lightly browned. Add onions, carrots, and celery; cook over medium heat until vegetables are tender, 15 to 20 minutes. Add lentils, ham hock, 8 cups water, bay leaf, salt, thyme, and pepper; heat to boiling over high heat. Reduce heat; cover and simmer until lentils are tender, 50 to 60 minutes. Remove and discard bay leaf.

2 Transfer ham hock to cutting board. Cut meat into bite-size pieces, discarding skin and bone. Return meat to soup. Heat through. Stir in lemon juice.

EACH SERVING: ABOUT 390 CALORIES, 25G PROTEIN, 52G CARBOHYDRATE, 10G TOTAL FAT (3G SATURATED), 19G FIBER, 1,027MG SODIUM.

From top: Squash Gazpacho, Fresh Melon Soup, Sweet Beet Soup (pages 105, 120, 111)

5 | Chilled

Who said soup was only for the fall and winter months? These chilled soups with fun and fruity flavors are the perfect refreshment on a warm day. Use garden-fresh vegetables for a summertime favorite like Gazpacho. Puree cool cucumbers and top with homemade curry oil for a delightful seasonal treat. Additionally, juicy cantaloupe makes a great base for a Fresh Melon Soup with Crispy Pancetta. Best served chilled, these soups celebrate the summer season.

Gazpacho

This chilled soup of Spanish origin combines ripe tomatoes
with other favorite veggies from the garden.

PREP: 30 MINUTES PLUS CHILLING
MAKES: 6 FIRST-COURSE SERVINGS

2   medium cucumbers (about 8 ounces each),
    peeled and seeded

2   pounds ripe tomatoes (about 6 medium),
    seeded and chopped

½   medium red bell pepper, coarsely chopped

1   garlic clove, chopped

3   tablespoons fresh lemon juice

1   tablespoon olive oil

1   teaspoon salt

⅛   teaspoon ground black pepper

1   cup corn kernels cut from cobs

1   avocado, cut into ½-inch pieces

¼   cup thinly sliced red onion

1 Cut 1 cucumber into ¼-inch pieces; cut remaining cucumber into chunks.

2 Spoon half of tomatoes, red bell pepper, garlic, lemon juice, oil, salt, black pepper, cucumber chunks, and ¼ cup water into blender; puree until smooth. Pour into large bowl. Repeat with remaining half and another ¼ cup water.

3 Stir in diced cucumber. Cover and refrigerate until well chilled, about 3 hours or overnight.

4 To serve, top soup with corn, avocado, and onion.

EACH SERVING: ABOUT 145 CALORIES, 3G PROTEIN, 19G CARBOHYDRATE, 8G TOTAL FAT (1G SATURATED), 5G FIBER, 470MG SODIUM.

Squash GAZPACHO

This summertime classic is only made better with summer's finest squash. For photo, see page 102.

PREP: 20 MINUTES PLUS CHILLING **COOK:** 25 MINUTES
MAKES: 4 FIRST-COURSE SERVINGS

2   tablespoons olive oil

1½   pounds yellow squash, seeded and sliced

1   large yellow bell pepper, seeded and sliced

2   garlic cloves, chopped

1   teaspoon ground cumin

1   teaspoon salt

2   cups lower-sodium vegetable or chicken broth, or 2 cups Vegetable Broth (page 14) or Chicken Broth (page 38)

1   tablespoon fresh lemon juice

4   ounces soft goat cheese

8   slices baguette, toasted

Smoked paprika, for garnish

1 In 5-quart saucepot, heat oil over medium heat. Add squash, bell pepper, garlic, cumin, and salt. Cook 10 minutes or until vegetables are almost soft, stirring occasionally.

2 Add broth to saucepot and heat to simmering on high. Reduce heat to medium; simmer 15 minutes or until vegetables are very soft.

3 Pour soup into blender; blend until smooth. Stir in lemon juice. Refrigerate until cold, about 8 hours.

4 When ready to serve, spread goat cheese on toasted baguette slices. Serve soup with goat cheese toasts and garnish with a pinch of smoked paprika.

EACH SERVING: ABOUT 255 CALORIES, 11G PROTEIN, 26G CARBOHYDRATE, 13G TOTAL FAT (5G SATURATED), 4G FIBER, 945MG SODIUM.

WHITE **Gazpacho**

Country white bread, cucumber, green grapes, and almonds
give this blender dinner its rich texture and signature hue.

PREP: 25 MINUTES PLUS 4 HOURS OR OVERNIGHT TO CHILL
MAKES: 4 FIRST-COURSE SERVINGS

6   thick slices country white bread, crusts removed and cut into 1-inch cubes (about 4 cups)

1   large seedless (English) cucumber, peeled and sliced

2   cups seedless green grapes

½   cup blanched almonds

2   small garlic cloves, peeled

Salt

2   teaspoons sherry vinegar

¼   cup, plus 2 tablespoons extra virgin olive oil

2   ripe medium tomatoes, cut in half

8   slices country white bread, toasted

1 In medium bowl, soak bread cubes in ½ cup cold water; set aside.

2 In blender, pulse cucumber, grapes, almonds, garlic, 1½ cups cold water, and 1½ teaspoons salt until finely chopped. Add soaked bread; puree until smooth. Pulse in vinegar and ¼ cup olive oil. Refrigerate until cold, at least 4 hours or up to 24 hours.

3 With box grater set in large bowl, grate tomatoes. Discard skins. To tomato pulp, add remaining 2 tablespoons oil and pinch salt. To serve, divide gazpacho among bowls. Garnish with additional oil and chopped almonds, if desired. Spoon tomato mixture onto toasts. Serve with gazpacho.

EACH SERVING: ABOUT 705 CALORIES, 14G PROTEIN, 80G CARBOHYDRATE, 36G TOTAL FAT (4G SATURATED), 1G FIBER, 715MG SODIUM.

Watermelon & Crab
GAZPACHO

This chilled soup delivers a fresh taste of summer, combining in-season produce like watermelon, zucchini, tomato, and basil.

PREP: 25 MINUTES PLUS 4 HOURS OR OVERNIGHT TO CHILL
MAKES: 4 FIRST-COURSE SERVINGS

2   pounds ripe tomatoes, cut in quarters

1/4   cup packed fresh basil leaves, plus additional for garnish

1/4   cup red wine vinegar

5   cups cubed seedless watermelon (from about 3 pounds watermelon with rind)

2   small garlic cloves

1/3   cup, plus 1 tablespoon extra virgin olive oil

1/2   teaspoon salt

1/4   teaspoon ground black pepper

1   small zucchini (4 ounces), finely chopped

1   small loaf French bread (4 ounces), cut into 8 slices

1   cup lump crabmeat, picked over

1 In food processor with knife blade attached, pulse tomatoes, basil leaves, vinegar, 4 cups watermelon cubes, 1 garlic clove, 1/3 cup oil, salt, and pepper until pureed.

2 Set medium-mesh sieve over medium bowl. Pour watermelon mixture through sieve, pressing on solids to extract all liquid; discard solids. Cover and refrigerate at least 4 hours and up to overnight. Place chopped zucchini and remaining 1 cup watermelon in another bowl; cover and refrigerate overnight.

3 To serve, cut remaining garlic clove in half. Lightly rub cut halves on bread slices. Brush remaining tablespoon oil on bread slices. Toast in toaster oven or broiler until golden brown and crisp.

4 Divide soup among 4 serving bowls. Top with zucchini, watermelon, and crab. Garnish with basil leaves. Serve gazpacho with garlic toasts.

EACH SERVING: ABOUT 410 CALORIES, 12G PROTEIN, 39G CARBOHYDRATE, 24G TOTAL FAT (3G SATURATED), 2G FIBER, 570MG SODIUM.

Chilled Cucumber
SOUP

Homemade curry oil adds a taste of southeast
Asia to this summer favorite.

PREP: 25 MINUTES PLUS CHILLING **COOK:** 3 MINUTES
MAKES: 4 FIRST-COURSE SERVINGS

Cucumber Soup

2 English (seedless) cucumbers
(about 12 ounces each), peeled

1 small garlic clove, crushed with garlic press

1 container (16 ounces) plain low-fat yogurt
(about 2 cups)

½ cup low-fat (1%) milk

1 tablespoon fresh lemon juice

1¼ teaspoons salt

Curry Oil

2 tablespoons olive oil

½ teaspoon curry powder

½ teaspoon ground cumin

¼ teaspoon crushed red pepper

Garnish

1 small tomato, chopped

1 tablespoon chopped fresh mint

1 Prepare soup: Cut enough cucumber into
¼-inch pieces to equal ½ cup; reserve for garnish.
Cut remaining cucumber into 1-inch pieces. In
food processor with knife blade attached, or in
blender, puree cucumber chunks, garlic, yogurt,
milk, lemon juice, and salt until almost smooth.
Pour mixture into medium bowl; cover and
refrigerate until cold, about 2 hours.

2 Prepare curry oil: In small saucepan, heat oil,
curry powder, cumin, and crushed red pepper
over low heat until fragrant and oil is hot, about
3 minutes. Remove saucepan from heat; strain
curry oil through sieve into cup.

3 Prepare garnish: In small bowl, combine
tomato and reserved cucumber pieces.

4 To serve, stir soup and ladle into 4 bowls. Spoon
cucumber mixture into center of soup. Sprinkle
with mint and drizzle with curry oil.

EACH SERVING: ABOUT 170 CALORIES, 8G PROTEIN,
15G CARBOHYDRATE, 9G TOTAL FAT (2G SATURATED),
1G FIBER, 830MG SODIUM.

Sweet Beet
SOUP

Tart Granny Smith apples brighten up this sweet
and savory soup. For photo, see page 102.

PREP: 15 MINUTES PLUS CHILLING   **COOK:** 5 MINUTES
MAKES: 4 FIRST-COURSE SERVINGS

1   tablespoon olive oil

1   medium onion, thinly sliced

Salt

1   pound cooked beets, refrigerated

1   Granny Smith apple, peeled, cored and
    chopped

2   cups lower-sodium vegetable or chicken
    broth, or 2 cups Vegetable Broth (page 14)
    or Chicken Broth (page 38)

Sour cream and dill, for garnish

1 In 10-inch skillet, heat oil over medium-high
heat. Add onion and a pinch of salt. Cook
5 minutes or until browned and starting to
soften, stirring frequently. Let cool.

2 To blender, add beets, apple, broth, onion, and
½ teaspoon salt. Blend until smooth. Refrigerate
until cold, about 3 hours. To serve, garnish with
sour cream and dill.

EACH SERVING: ABOUT 120 CALORIES, 2G PROTEIN,
21G CARBOHYDRATE, 4G TOTAL FAT (1G SATURATED),
3G FIBER, 580MG SODIUM.

Vichyssoise

This luxurious soup, traditionally served cold, is just as delicious hot. Either way, serve in small cups and garnish with freshly chopped chives.

PREP: 20 MINUTES PLUS CHILLING   **COOK:** 55 MINUTES
MAKES: 8 FIRST-COURSE SERVINGS

4 medium leeks (1¼ pounds)

2 tablespoons butter or margarine

1 pound all-purpose potatoes (3 medium), peeled and thinly sliced

2 cans (14 to 14½ ounces each) chicken broth or 3½ cups Chicken Broth (page 38)

1 teaspoon salt

¼ teaspoon ground black pepper

1 cup milk

½ cup heavy or whipping cream

Chives, for garnish

1 Cut off roots and trim dark green tops from leeks; cut each leek lengthwise in half. Cut enough of white and pale green parts crosswise into ¼-inch pieces to equal 4½ cups. (Reserve any leftover leeks for another use.) Rinse leeks in large bowl of cold water, swishing to remove sand. Transfer to colander to drain, leaving sand in bottom of bowl.

2 In nonreactive 4-quart saucepan, melt butter over medium heat. Add leeks and cook, stirring occasionally, 8 to 10 minutes.

3 Add potatoes, broth, ½ cup water, salt, and pepper; heat to boiling over high heat. Reduce heat; cover and simmer 30 minutes.

4 Spoon half of mixture into blender; cover, with center part of lid removed to let steam escape, and puree until smooth. Pour into bowl. Repeat with remaining mixture.

5 Stir milk and cream into puree. To serve hot, return soup to same clean saucepan and heat through over low heat (do not boil). To serve cold, cover and refrigerate at least 4 hours or until very cold. Garnish with chives before serving.

EACH SERVING: ABOUT 161 CALORIES, 4G PROTEIN, 14G CARBOHYDRATE, 10G TOTAL FAT (7G SATURATED), 2G FIBER, 769MG SODIUM.

Chilled Buttermilk-Vegetable
SOUP

The refreshing, cool flavors of summer vegetables make
this chunky soup a delightful first course.

PREP: 20 MINUTES PLUS CHILLING
MAKES: 10 FIRST-COURSE SERVINGS

2   limes

1½ quarts buttermilk (6 cups)

3   medium tomatoes (about 1 pound), seeded
    and cut into ¼-inch pieces

1   English (seedless) cucumber, unpeeled and
    cut into ¼-inch pieces

1   ripe avocado, cut into ¼-inch pieces

1   cup loosely packed fresh cilantro, chopped

1   teaspoon salt

¼   teaspoon ground black pepper

Fresh cilantro sprigs, for garnish

1 From limes, grate 1 teaspoon peel and squeeze
3 tablespoons juice.

2 In large bowl, combine lime peel and juice,
buttermilk, tomatoes, cucumber, avocado,
cilantro, salt, and pepper and stir until blended.
Cover and refrigerate at least 2 hours or up to
1 day. Garnish each serving with a cilantro sprig.

EACH SERVING: ABOUT 105 CALORIES, 6G PROTEIN,
11G CARBOHYDRATE, 4G TOTAL FAT (1G SATURATED),
2G FIBER, 395MG SODIUM.

Spicy Gazpacho with
SERRANO HAM

Dig into chilled summer soup with a spicy kick.

PREP: 25 MINUTES PLUS CHILLING
MAKES: 4 MAIN-DISH SERVINGS

- 3 cups torn or cubed stale country white bread, crusts removed
- 3 pounds ripe tomatoes, cored and coarsely chopped
- 4 serrano chiles, sliced
- 3 garlic cloves, coarsely chopped
- 3/4 cups extra virgin olive oil, plus more for garnish
- 5 teaspoons sherry vinegar
- 1 teaspoon salt
- 2 ounces serrano ham, thinly sliced into strips
- Chopped fresh parsley, for garnish

1 In a medium bowl, cover bread with enough cold water to soak. Let stand 15 minutes. Drain well and squeeze out excess water.

2 In a food processor, blend half the tomatoes, serranos, garlic, oil, and soaked bread until smooth, stopping and scraping occasionally. Transfer to 8-cup measuring cup or other large container. Repeat blending with remaining tomatoes, chiles, garlic, bread, and oil; add to measuring cup with first batch of soup. Stir in vinegar and salt. Cover with plastic wrap and refrigerate until cold, about 3 hours or up to 1 day. Divide among serving bowls. Drizzle with additional oil, if desired. Garnish with ham and parsley.

EACH SERVING: ABOUT 545 CALORIES, 9G PROTEIN, 28G CARBOHYDRATE, 45G TOTAL FAT (7G SATURATED), 5G FIBER, 990MG SODIUM.

TIP
Want to turn up the heat? Drizzle with chile oil. Want cool it down? Replace the serrano chiles with 1 cubanelle pepper.

Chilled Corn &
BACON SOUP

This refreshing farm-stand soup is August's answer to cold-weather chowders—thickened with late-season corn, low-fat milk, and a Yukon gold potato.

PREP: 15 MINUTES PLUS CHILLING   **COOK:** 20 MINUTES
MAKES: 4 FIRST-COURSE SERVINGS

4   slices thick-cut bacon, cut into ½-inch pieces

1   large shallot, finely chopped

3   cups fresh corn kernels

1   large Yukon gold potato (8 ounces), peeled and shredded

⅛   teaspoon smoked paprika, plus additional for garnish

4   cups low-fat (1%) milk

⅛   teaspoon salt

⅛   teaspoon ground black pepper

¼   cup packed fresh cilantro leaves

1 In 12-inch skillet, cook bacon over medium heat 6 to 8 minutes or until crisp and browned. With slotted spoon, transfer to paper towels to drain. If making ahead, cover and refrigerate up to overnight.

2 Drain and discard all but 1 tablespoon fat from skillet. Add shallots and cook over medium heat 2 minutes or until golden and tender, stirring occasionally. Add 2½ cups corn, shredded potato, and paprika. Cook 2 minutes, stirring, then add ⅔ cup water and cook 7 minutes or until liquid evaporates and vegetables are tender.

3 Remove skillet from heat and transfer corn mixture to blender. Add milk and salt and puree until mixture is very smooth. Cover and refrigerate until soup is very cold, at least 3 hours and up to overnight.

4 To serve, divide among serving bowls. Top with bacon, cilantro, pepper, and remaining ½ cup corn. Garnish with paprika.

....

EACH SERVING: ABOUT 375 CALORIES, 17G PROTEIN, 54G CARBOHYDRATE, 12G TOTAL FAT (5G SATURATED), 5G FIBER, 750MG SODIUM.

Chilled Tuscan-Style
TOMATO SOUP

The lush summer flavors of Tuscany shine in this cold tomato soup.
We blend country bread with tomatoes to achieve
a thicker body and a velvety mouthfeel.

PREP: 15 MINUTES PLUS CHILLING
MAKES: 4 FIRST-COURSE SERVINGS

1   teaspoon olive oil

1   garlic clove, minced

2   cups 1-inch country-style bread cubes

3   pounds ripe tomatoes, each cut into quarters

¼   cup loosely packed fresh basil leaves, chopped, plus additional basil leaves, for garnish

1   teaspoon sugar

½   teaspoon salt

1 In small skillet, heat oil over medium heat until hot. Add garlic and cook 1 minute, stirring. Remove skillet from heat.

2 In food processor with knife blade attached, pulse bread until coarsely chopped. Add tomatoes and garlic; pulse until soup is almost pureed. Pour soup into bowl; stir in chopped basil, sugar, and salt. Cover and refrigerate until well chilled, at least 2 hours or overnight. Garnish each serving with basil leaves.

EACH SERVING: ABOUT 145 CALORIES, 5G PROTEIN, 28G CARBOHYDRATE, 3G TOTAL FAT (1G SATURATED), 4G FIBER, 445MG SODIUM

Chilled Caprese
SOUP

With all of the ingredients of a caprese salad, this soup is a perfectly refreshing new take on an old classic. For photo, see page 6.

PREP: 15 MINUTES PLUS CHILLING   **COOK:** 16 MINUTES
MAKES: 4 MAIN-DISH SERVINGS

3   cups ½-inch bread cubes, preferably country-style bread

3   pounds tomatoes, cored, seeded, and cut into quarters

1   tablespoon sherry or red wine vinegar

2   small garlic cloves, peeled

Salt

¼   teaspoon ground black pepper

¼   cup extra virgin olive oil

¼   cup packed fresh basil leaves, finely chopped

4   ounces fresh mozzarella cheese, cut into ¼-inch cubes

¼   cup seedless (English) cucumber, finely chopped

¼   cup green bell pepper, finely chopped

1 Preheat oven to 350°F. In a medium bowl, soak 1½ cups bread cubes in 1 cup warm water. Meanwhile, arrange remaining 1½ cups bread in jelly-roll pan and bake 16 minutes or until golden.
2 Working in batches, squeeze excess water from soaked bread cubes and transfer to food processor. Add tomatoes, vinegar, 1 garlic clove, ½ teaspoon salt, and pepper; pulse until almost smooth. Refrigerate until cold, about 2 hours.
3 Meanwhile, with garlic press, press remaining clove into medium bowl; whisk in olive oil, basil, and ⅛ teaspoon salt.
4 To serve, add toasted bread cubes to basil-oil mixture; toss to coat. Stir in mozzarella, cucumber, and green pepper. Divide chilled soup among 4 bowls and top with mozzarella mixture.

EACH SERVING: ABOUT 350 CALORIES, 10G PROTEIN, 29G CARBOHYDRATE, 22G TOTAL FAT (6G SATURATED), 5G FIBER, 580MG SODIUM

TIP
Want to take it a little south-of-the-border instead? Swap in pepper Jack cheese for the mozzarella and fresh cilantro for the basil.

Fresh Melon Soup with
CRISPY PANCETTA

Kick up this cool summer soup with some crispy pancetta.
For photo, see page 102.

PREP: 20 MINUTES PLUS CHILLING COOK: 15 MINUTES
MAKES: 4 FIRST-COURSE OR DESSERT SERVINGS

2 small ripe cantaloupes, peeled, seeded, and chopped

¼ cup fresh lemon juice

1 teaspoon salt

¼ cup packed fresh basil leaves

½ cup olive oil

1 tablespoon snipped chives, plus more for garnish

8 thin slices pancetta

Ground black pepper

1 In blender, combine cantaloupe, lemon juice, 1¼ cups water, and salt. Blend until smooth. Refrigerate until cold, about 2 hours. (Can be made up to 2 days ahead; refrigerate.)

2 Heat a 2-quart saucepan of water to boiling on high. Fill bowl with ice water. Add basil to boiling water; boil 30 seconds or until bright green. With slotted spoon, transfer basil to bowl with ice water. Let stand 5 minutes; drain thoroughly. Pat basil dry. To blender, add basil, oil, and chives. Blend until smooth; set aside.

3 Preheat oven to 400°F. Line rimmed baking sheet with foil. Arrange pancetta in single layer. Bake 14 to 16 minutes or until golden brown. Transfer to paper towel.

4 To serve, divide soup among serving bowls. Top each with herb oil, pinch black pepper, chives, and pancetta.

EACH SERVING: ABOUT 335 CALORIES, 3G PROTEIN, 19G CARBOHYDRATE, 29G TOTAL FAT (4G SATURATED), 2G FIBER, 680MG SODIUM.

Fruit Soup with
COCONUT SORBET

This luscious soup is delightful at either the beginning or the end of a meal.

PREP: 10 MINUTES PLUS CHILLING
MAKES: 4 CUPS OR 4 SERVINGS

1   lime

1   bottle (1 pint) passion fruit juice blend

2   tablespoons sugar

1   large ripe peach, peeled, pitted, and thinly sliced

1   red plum, pitted and thinly sliced

½   cup blueberries

½   cup raspberries

1   pint coconut, passion fruit, or mango sorbet

Mint sprigs, for garnish

1 From lime, grate ½ teaspoon peel and squeeze 2 tablespoons juice.

2 In medium bowl, toss lime peel and juice, fruit juice, sugar, peach, plum, blueberries, and raspberries until mixed. Cover and refrigerate at least 2 hours or until cold.

3 To serve, ladle fruit mixture into 4 shallow soup bowls. Top each with a scoop of sorbet. Garnish with mint sprigs.

EACH SERVING: ABOUT 240 CALORIES, 0G PROTEIN, 55G CARBOHYDRATE, 3G TOTAL FAT (2G SATURATED), 2G FIBER, 40MG SODIUM.

Pear & Red Wine
SOUP

Serve this chilled soup before a hearty main course. As with all fruit soups, make it with fully ripened fruit at its peak of flavor.

PREP: 10 MINUTES PLUS CHILLING   **COOK:** 20 TO 25 MINUTES
MAKES: 4 FIRST-COURSE SERVINGS

1   cup dry red wine

⅓   cup sugar

1   lemon

1⅓   pounds ripe pears, peeled, cored, and cut into quarters

1 In nonreactive 2-quart saucepan, heat wine, 1 cup water, and sugar to boiling over high heat, stirring frequently, until sugar has dissolved.

2 Meanwhile, with vegetable peeler, remove two 3-inch strips peel from lemon; squeeze 1 tablespoon juice.

3 Add pears and lemon peel to saucepan; heat to boiling over high heat. Reduce heat and simmer until pears are very tender, 10 to 15 minutes.

4 Spoon one-fourth of pear mixture into blender; cover, with center part of lid removed to let steam escape, and puree until smooth. Pour puree into bowl. Repeat with remaining mixture. Stir in lemon juice. Cover soup and refrigerate at least 4 hours or until very cold.

EACH SERVING: ABOUT 234 CALORIES, 1G PROTEIN, 50G CARBOHYDRATE, 1G TOTAL FAT (0G SATURATED), 3G FIBER, 3MG SODIUM.

Honeydew & Lime
SOUP

This chilled soup starts a summer meal off with a refreshing mix of surprising flavors. Choose a melon that is fully ripe for a smooth consistency.

PREP: 10 MINUTES PLUS CHILLING
MAKES: 6 FIRST-COURSE SERVINGS

1   honeydew melon (5 pounds), chilled, cut into 1-inch chunks (8 cups)

¼   cup fresh lime juice

¼   cup loosely packed fresh cilantro leaves

1   teaspoon jalapeño hot sauce

⅛   teaspoon salt

In blender, pulse melon with lime juice, cilantro, hot sauce, and salt until pureed. Transfer soup to large bowl or pitcher; cover and refrigerate 2 hours or until chilled. Stir before serving.

EACH SERVING: ABOUT 85 CALORIES, 1G PROTEIN, 23G CARBOHYDRATE, 0G TOTAL FAT (0G SATURATED), 2G FIBER, 80MG SODIUM.

Index

Note: Page numbers in *italics* indicate photos on pages separate from recipes.

Photo Credits

Metric Conversion Charts

The recipes that appear in this cookbook use the standard U.S. method for measuring liquid and dry or solid ingredients (teaspoons, tablespoons, and cups). The information on this chart is provided to help cooks outside the United States successfully use these recipes. All equivalents are approximate.

METRIC EQUIVALENTS FOR DIFFERENT TYPES OF INGREDIENTS

STANDARD CUP	FINE POWDER (e.g., flour)	GRAIN (e.g., rice)	GRANULAR (e.g., sugar)	LIQUID SOLIDS (e.g., butter)	LIQUID (e.g., milk)
¾	105 g	113 g	143 g	150 g	180 ml
⅔	93 g	100 g	125 g	133 g	160 ml
½	70 g	75 g	95 g	100 g	120 ml
⅓	47 g	50 g	63 g	67 g	80 ml
¼	35 g	38 g	48 g	50 g	60 ml
⅛	18 g	19 g	24 g	25 g	30 ml

USEFUL EQUIVALENTS FOR LIQUID INGREDIENTS BY VOLUME

¼ tsp	=						1 ml
½ tsp	=						2 ml
1 tsp	=						5 ml
3 tsp	=	1 tbsp	=		½ fl oz	=	15 ml
		2 tbsp	=	⅛ cup	1 fl oz	=	30 ml
		4 tbsp	=	¼ cup	2 fl oz	=	60 ml
		5⅓ tbsp	=	⅓ cup	3 fl oz	=	80 ml
		8 tbsp	=	½ cup	4 fl oz	=	120 ml
		10⅔ tbsp	=	⅔ cup	5 fl oz	=	160 ml
		12 tbsp	=	¾ cup	6 fl oz	=	180 ml
		16 tbsp	=	1 cup	8 fl oz	=	240 ml
		1 pt	=	2 cups	16 fl oz	=	480 ml
		1 qt	=	4 cups	32 fl oz	=	960 ml
					33 fl oz	=	1000 ml = 1 L

USEFUL EQUIVALENTS FOR DRY INGREDIENTS BY WEIGHT

(To convert ounces to grams, multiply the number of ounces by 30.)

1 oz	=	¹⁄₁₆ lb	=	30 g
4 oz	=	¼ lb	=	120 g
8 oz	=	½ lb	=	240 g
12 oz	=	¾ lb	=	360 g
16 oz	=	1 lb	=	480 g

USEFUL EQUIVALENTS FOR COOKING/OVEN TEMPERATURES

	Fahrenheit	Celsius	Gas Mark
Freeze Water	32°F	0°C	
Room Temperature	68°F	20°C	
Boil Water	212°F	100°C	
Bake	325°F	160°C	3
	350°F	180°C	4
	375°F	190°C	5
	400°F	200°C	6
	425°F	220°C	7
	450°F	230°C	8
Broil			Grill

USEFUL EQUIVALENTS LENGTH

(To convert inches to centimeters, multiply the number of inches by 2.5.)

1 in	=			2.5 cm
6 in	=	½ ft	=	15 cm
12 in	=	1 ft	=	30 cm
36 in	=	3 ft	= 1 yd	= 90 cm
40 in	=			100 cm = 1 m

THE GOOD HOUSEKEEPING
TRIPLE-TEST PROMISE

At Good Housekeeping, we want to make sure that every recipe we print works in any oven, with any brand of ingredient, no matter what. That's why, in our test kitchens at the **Good Housekeeping Research Institute**, we go all out: We test each recipe at least three times—and, often, several more times after that.

When a recipe is first developed, one member of our team prepares the dish, and we judge it on these criteria: It must be **delicious**, **family-friendly**, **healthy**, and **easy to make**.

1 The recipe is then tested several more times to fine-tune the flavor and ease of preparation, always by the same team member, using the same equipment.

2 Next, another team member follows the recipe as written, **varying the brands of ingredients** and **kinds of equipment**. Even the types of stoves we use are changed.

3 A third team member repeats the whole process **using yet another set of equipment** and **alternative ingredients**. By the time the recipes appear on these pages, they are guaranteed to work in any kitchen, including yours. **We promise.**